A Bark In The Park -

The 40 Best Places To Hike With Your Dog In The Reno/Lake Tahoe Region

SHERRIL STEELE-CARLIN

illustrations by
ANDREW CHESWORTH

Cruden Bay Books

A BARK IN THE PARK: THE 40 BEST PLACES TO
HIKE WITH YOUR DOG IN THE RENO/LAKE TAHOE
REGION

Copyright 2003 by Sherril Steele-Carlin

Cruden Bay Books
PO Box 467
Montchanin, DE 19710

www.hikewithyourdog.com

International Standard Book Number 0-9744083-0-1

Manufactured in the United States of America

A Bark In The Park -

The 40 Best Places To Hike With Your Dog In The Reno/Lake Tahoe Region

"Dogs are our link to paradise...to sit with a dog on a hillside on a glorious afternoon is to be back in Eden, where doing nothing was not boring - it was peace."
- Milan Kundera

Contents

Also...

Introduction

The Reno and Lake Tahoe areas are amazing places to explore hiking trails with your dog. The area is so diverse, you can experience high-mountain trails, sandy desert paths, and leisurely river walks, all within an hour or so drive from each other. Along the way, you can discover the region's varied history, from old mining towns to blackjack tables, all the while taking in the clean, fresh air of the High Sierra. The air is a little crisper in this high altitude, and the sky is definitely bluer. It is the perfect place to see the sights on foot, whether you are a novice canine hiker or a seasoned professional, there are trails for every dog!

This book highlights the 40 best parks in the Reno and Lake Tahoe region where you can enjoy a day out with your dog. I have ranked them according to subjective criteria, including the variety of hiking available in each park, scenic beauty, opportunities for your dog to swim, their proximity to Reno, and the pleasure of the walks. The rankings include a mix of parks featuring long rambles along with parks that contain short walks. I've also included another list of 50 other great places to walk your dog.

For dog owners it is important to realize that not all parks are open to our dogs (see page 115 for a list of parks that do not allow dogs). Thankfully, there are only a handful of parks in the area that ban our friends! Rules pertaining to dogs in parks can change rapidly, so it's always a good idea to check with a park beforehand if you are not sure about your dog's being welcome. Please be aware that when you visit a California State Park, you will need a rabies certificate or dog license to bring a dog into a State Park, and dogs are not allowed on the trails or beaches in local California State Parks.

When you visit a park, don't forget to keep your dog under control and clean up any messes, or more and more area parks will be closed to dogs. Most of the dogparks listed in this book provide plastic gloves and waste receptacles for doggie messes, be sure to use them.

So grab that leash and hit the trail!

Hiking With Your Dog

So you want to start hiking with your dog. Hiking with your dog can be a fascinating way to explore the region around Reno and Lake Tahoe from a canine perspective. Some things to consider:

🐾 Dog's Health

Hiking can be a wonderful preventative for any number of physical and behavioral disorders. One in every three dogs is overweight and running up trails is great exercise to help keep pounds off. Hiking can also relieve boredom in a dog's routine and calm dogs prone to destructive habits. And hiking with your dog strengthens the overall owner/dog bond.

🐾 Breed of Dog

All dogs enjoy the new scents and sights of a trail. But some dogs are better suited to hiking than others. If you don't as yet have a hiking companion, select a breed that matches your interests. Do you look forward to an entire afternoon's hiking? You'll need a dog bred to keep up with such a pace, a retriever or a spaniel for instance. Is a half-hour enough walking for you? It may not be for an energetic dog like a border collie. If you already have a hiking friend, tailor your plans to his abilities.

🐾 Conditioning

Just like humans, dogs need to be acclimated to the task at hand. An inactive dog cannot be expected to bounce from the easy chair in the den to complete a 3-hour hike. You must also be physically able to restrain your dog if confronted with distractions on the trail (like a scampering squirrel or a pack of joggers). Have your dog checked by a veterinarian before significantly increasing her activity level.

🐾 Weather

Heat and sun do dogs no favors. While the weather in Reno and Lake Tahoe is rarely very humid, the summer temperatures can reach over 100 degrees in the valleys. With no sweat glands and only panting available to disperse body heat, dogs are much more susceptible to heat stroke than we are. Unusually rapid panting and/or a bright red tongue are signs of heat exhaustion in your pet. Always carry enough water for your hike. Even days that don't seem too warm can cause discomfort in dark-coated dogs if the sun is shining brightly. In the wintertime, temperatures at these higher elevations can drop well below zero in only a few minutes. In cold weather, short-coated breeds may require additional attention.

🐾 Ticks

Lyme disease rarely occurs in the Northern Nevada area. The first reported case in Washoe County occurred in 2001. Lyme disease attacks a dog's joints and makes walking painful. The good news is that a tick needs to be embedded in the skin to transmit Lyme disease. It takes 4-6 hours for a tick to become embedded and another 24-48 hours to transmit the Lyme disease bacteria. When hiking, walk in the middle of trails away from tall grass and bushes. If your walk includes fields or meadows, consider long sleeves and long pants tucked into high socks. Wear a hat - ticks like hair. By checking your dog, and yourself, thoroughly after each walk, you can help avoid Lyme disease. Ticks tend to congregate on your dog's ears, between the toes, and around the neck and head.

🐾 Altitude

Altitude is a big factor when you hike in the Reno and Lake Tahoe areas. The Reno area is not quite 5,000 feet in altitude, and as you climb into the foothills, you will quickly hike above one mile in elevation. If you are hiking at Lake Tahoe, the altitude starts at over 6,000 feet, and many of the trails included here top out at 7,000 or 8,000 feet, or even higher. If you are not acclimated to the altitude, take it easy, and allow plenty of time for rest, so your body can get used to the thinner air up here.

🐾 Bears

Yes, there are bears in Northern Nevada. We don't see them often, but they are there, and you need to be aware of them. Once in a while in drought years we see a stray bear in Reno, but most of the time they stay in the high country around Lake Tahoe. Tahoe has experienced problems with bears getting into garbage but they are rarely seen on hiking trails. Just in case, there are some things you can do to make sure you and your dog don't have a run in with a bear.

First, it is a good idea to contact the local Forest Service or Fish and Game Department to find out about recent bear activity in the area where you plan to hike. If you take food along, don't pack in smelly, greasy foods like bacon and fish. Bears are most active in the cooler parts of the day, so avoid hiking at dawn and dusk, and you'll have less chance of encountering a hungry bear. They scatter at the sound of noise so tying a bell on your dog's collar can scare away a bear, and let you know where he is right away. If you should stumble across a bear on the trail be aware that you will not outrun a bear and bears do climb trees. Try to remain calm, avoid direct contact, and back slowly out of the area. Keep your dog close at hand - dogs often antagonize bears.

🐾 Rattlesnakes

Rattlesnakes are a hazard on any Northern Nevada trail, especially in the spring and summer months. They often hide under large rocks and crevices, and their sandy coloring helps them blend in with their surroundings very well. A rattlesnake bite to a human is painful and dangerous, and even more dangerous for your dog.

In the heat of a summer day, snakes will probably be lounging in the shade, but even in winter they will come out on sunny days to warm themselves. If you run into a rattler on the trail, first, leave it alone. Snakes don't have to be coiled to strike, and they don't always rattle before they strike. Snakes can't see well, so they will simply react to anything unknown by defending themselves. Don't go reaching under rocks, crevices, or loose pieces of wood without looking for snakes first. Don't let your dog nose around in those areas, either. Walk "heavy." Do not shuffle your steps when you walk in rattlesnake country. Snakes feel the vibrations if you put down your feet heavily, and will leave the area.

If your dog is bitten, go to your veterinarian immediately, and make sure they have antivenin on hand. This is the only thing that can save your pet in the event of a rattlesnake bite. Early morning and early evening hours are the most likely times to encounter snakes, they are more active during those times of the day. During the hottest parts of the day, snakes perfer to slumber. If you follow these precautions, your hike with your dog should be snake free. You can also sign up for a snake-avoidance course for your dog, sponsored by the Nevada Wildlife Federation and Reno's German Shorthaired Pointer Club. For more information, call Lorna Weaver at (775) 677-0927 or Quail Unlimited's Rudy Hindelang at (775) 267-5269. The course costs $50.

❖ Other Trail Hazards

Dogs won't get poison ivy but they can transfer it to you. Some trails are littered with small pieces of broken glass that can slice a dog's paws. Nasty thorns and thistles can also blanket trails that we in shoes may never notice. Tumbleweeds are also very thorny and prickly in their natural state, and even more so when they are dried and blowing. They can stick in a dog's coat, and cut fingers as we try to extract them.

❖ Water

Surface water, including fast-flowing streams, is likely to be infested with a microscopic protozoa called *Giardia*, waiting to wreck havoc on a dog's (and human's) intestinal system. (We call it "beaver fever" in Northern Nevada.) The most common symptom is crippling diarrhea. Algae, pollutants and contaminants can all be in streams, ponds and puddles. If possible, carry fresh water for your dog on the trail - your dog can even learn to drink happily from a squirt bottle.

With summer temperatures commonly reaching over 100 degrees on the valley floors, and 80 to 90 degrees in the upper elevations, water on the trail is a must in Northern Nevada, even for very short hikes. The humidity level is low, but the altitudes are 4,500 feet and up in Reno and Sparks and 7,000 feet or more at Lake Tahoe, so you and your pet may tire more easily, and need more water.

Outfitting Your Dog For A Hike

These are the basics for taking your dog on a hike:

▶ **Collar**. It should not be so loose as to come off but you should be able to slide your flat hand under collar.

▶ **Identification Tags**.

▶ **Bandanna**. Can help distinguish your dog from game in hunting season.

▶ **Leash**. Leather lasts forever but if there's water in your dog's future, consider quick-drying nylon.

🐾 *I want my dog to help carry water, snacks and other supplies on the trail. How do I choose a dog pack?*
To select an appropriate dog pack measure your dog's girth around the rib cage to determine the best pack size. A dog pack should fit securely without hindering the dog's ability to walk normally.

🐾 *How does a dog wear a pack?*
The pack, typically with cargo pouches on either side, should ride as close to the shoulders as possible without limiting movement. The straps that hold the dog pack in place should be situated where they will not cause chafing.

🐾 *Will my dog wear a pack?*
Wearing a dog pack is no more obtrusive than wearing a collar, although some dogs will take to a pack easier than others. Introduce the pack by draping a towel over your dog's back in the house and then having him wear an empty pack on short walks. Progressively add some crumpled newspaper and then bits of clothing. Fill the pack with treats and reward your dog from the stash. Soon he will associate the dog pack with an outdoor adventure and will eagerly look forward to wearing it.

🐾 *How much weight can I put into a dog pack?*

Many dog packs are sold by weight recommendations. A healthy, well-conditioned dog can comfortably carry 25 percent to 33 percent of its body weight. Breeds prone to back problems or hip dysplasia should not wear dog packs. Consult your veterinarian before stuffing the pouches with gear.

🐾 *What are good things to put in a dog pack?*

Low density items such as food and poop bags are good choices. Ice cold bottles of water can cool your dog down on hot days. Don't put anything in a dog pack that can break. Dogs will bang the pack on rocks and trees when they wiggle through tight spots in the trail. Dogs also like to lie down in creeks and other wet spots so seal items in plastic bags. A good use for dog packs on day hikes around Northern Nevada is trail maintenance - your dog can pack out trash left by inconsiderate visitors before you.

🐾 *Are dog booties a good idea?*

Dog booties can be an asset, especially for the occasional dog hiker whose paw pads have not become toughened. Many trails around Northern Nevada involve rocky terrain. In some places, broken glass abounds. Hiking boots for dogs are designed to prevent pads from cracking while trotting across rough surfaces. Used in winter, dog booties provide warmth and keep ice balls from forming between toe pads when hiking through snow.

"Dogs' lives are too short. Their only fault, really"
- Agnes Sligh Turnbull

The Canine First-Aid Hiking Kit

Even when taking short hikes it is a good idea to have some basics available for emergencies:

- Bandage material, vet wrap, cotton padding. If your dog burns or abrades his paws on hot or abrasive surfaces, you can pad his feet so he can walk.

- Antihistamine. If your dog is bitten by a snake or stung by a bee or wasp, administer antihistamine, about a milligram per pound.

- Cortisone tablets or aspirin as an anti-inflammatory. Also have a topical wound disinfectant cream available.

- Needle nose pliers. Use these for plucking out stickers or cactus spines.

- Petroleum jelly (to cover ticks).

- Your veterinarian's phone number.

*"If there are no dogs in Heaven,
then when I die I want to go where they went."*
- Anonymous

Low Impact Hiking With Your Dog

Everytime you hike with your dog on the trail, you are an ambassador for all dog owners. Some people you meet won't believe in your right to take a dog on the trail. Be friendly to all and make the best impression you can by practicing low impact hiking with your dog:

- Pack out everything you pack in.

- Do not leave dog scat on the trail; if you haven't brought plastic bags for poop removal bury it away from the trail and topical water sources.

- Hike only where dogs are allowed.

- Stay on the trail.

- Do not allow your dog to chase wildlife.

- Step off the trail and wait with your dog while horses and other hikers pass.

- Do not allow your dog to bark - people are enjoying the trail for serenity.

- Have as much fun on your hike as your dog does.

"What counts is not necessarily the size of the dog in the fight but the size of the fight in the dog."
- Dwight D. Eisenhower

Camping With Your Dog

Many of the parks in Northern Nevada and Lake Tahoe have campsites right there, along with miles of hiking trails, so it is natural you might want to spend the night after a long day on the trails. If you decide to camp with your dog, here are some tips:

- Camp only in areas that are approved by the U. S. Forest Service, Washoe County, or Bureau of Land Management (BLM).

- Be sure your dog is wearing I.D. tags, and has all current shots.

- Take along plenty of food and water.

- Have private sleeping arrangements, and camp in a shady area.

- Don't let your dog run loose in the campsite.

- If your dog swims, make sure he has a way out of the water. Dogs can drown because they try to climb out a bank or ledge that is too steep for them.

- Rinse off your dog with fresh water when you are done hiking and/or camping, and look for ticks and fleas.

Happiness is dog-shaped.
-Chapman Pincher

Summer Safety Tips For Your Dog

One of the biggest killers of dogs in hot weather is being left in a car for too long. Even as little as 10 minutes can be too long for a dog left in a closed car on a hot day. In that short a time, the inside temperature of the car could reach 160 degrees! Heat like that can cause heat stroke in your pet, and within moments it could cause permanent brain damage - and if you don't get your dog to a veterinarian fast enough, she could die. It is best to leave your dog at home if you are not going straight to the hiking trail and back again on hot summer days. Here are some more tips for summer safety:

- Make sure your dog has shade or shelter if he is outdoors during the day.

- Make sure there is plenty of fresh water to drink.

- Groom your dog's coat for summer weather.

- Protect against sunburn, especially on the nose and ears.

- Be careful of hot pavements on tender paw pads.

- Don't let your dog ride without a harness in the back of a pickup truck.

To err is human, to forgive, canine.
-anonymous

Skiing With Your Dog

In the Lake Tahoe area, many cross-country ski areas know that dogs love to ski just as much as their owners, and are allowing them on trails. If you would love to ski with your dog, here are some resorts that allow dogs on their trails. Many have specific times dogs are allowed, so call to find out the days and times you can bring your dog. There are also nominal fees for allowing your dog on the trails.

- **Tahoe Cross Country**
  (530) 583-5475 or http://www.tahoexc.org.

- **Royal Gorge Cross Country Resort**
  (800) 500-3871 or http://www.royalgorge.com.

- **Spooner Lake Cross Country**
  (888) 858-8844 or http://www.spoonerlake.com.

- **Hope Valley Cross Country**
  (530) 694-2266 or http://www.sorensonsresort.com.

- **Kirkwood Cross Country**
  (209) 258-7248 or http://www.skikirkwood.com.

Dogs are also welcome on many Forest Service ski trails: Taylor Creek, Echo Lakes, Grass Lake Meadow, Angora Road, and Fallen Leaf Lake. See the entries for these hikes, and follow the same directions to find the cross-country ski areas.

Skijoring
If your dog is 35 pounds or up, you might enjoy trying Skijoring, a Norwegian sport where skiers in a special sled are pulled by their dog over the snow. You can find out more about this sport at: http://www.ptialaska.net/~skijor/. Skijoring lessons are offered at Royal Gorge Cross Country Ski Resort or from Debbie McMaster at Sierra Ski Joring (530) 587-2732.

Special Dog Events in Reno and Lake Tahoe

🐾 Art Paws in the Park

During Artown, a month-long celebration of the arts in Reno each July, a local art gallery sponsors "Art Paws in the Park." This fanciful event is an art fair for dogs (and their owners). One booth features pen and ink drawings of your pet while you wait; another allows your dog to get her paws wet and paint her own masterwork. There is also a pet psychic on hand to "talk" to your dog, a booth where you can create customized placemats for your dog, an agility course, and much more. Some events are free and some require a donation, which benefits a local organizations. To find out more about the current Art Paws in the Park, call Artown at (775) 322-1538.

🐾 4 Paws Festival

The Reno Society for the Protection of Animals (SPCA) holds these festivals throughout the year. Dogs and their owners are welcome to take part in a "pooch parade." You can also enjoy food and drinks, live music, and adopt animals. Call (775) 324-7773 or visit the website for more information: http://spcaofnn.org.

🐾 Snowfest

Each March, North Lake Tahoe sponsors a fantastic snow festival called Snowfest. During this 10-day celebration, there are several dog events scheduled so your pet can also join in the fun. The "Nawty Dawg" sponsors the "Monstor Dawg Pull," and there is a "Dress up Your Dog" contest. Call (530) 581-1283 for more information about the current festival.

The Other End Of The Leash

Leash laws are like speed limits - everyone seems to have a private interpretation of their validity. Some dog owners never go outside with an unleashed dog; others treat the laws as suggestions or disregard them completely. It is not the purpose of this book to tell dog owners where to go to evade the leash laws or reveal the parks where rangers will look the other way at an unleashed dog. Nor is it the business of this book to preach vigilant adherence to the leash laws. Nothing written in a book is going to change people's behavior with regard to leash laws. So this will be the last time leash laws are mentioned, save occasionally when I point out the parks where dogs are welcomed off leash.

As a general rule, dogs should be kept on a leash in all city and state parks. (You will be fined if caught violating this rule.) On land managed by the Bureau of Land Management (clearly indicated in each hike), you may let dogs off the leash unless otherwise indicated at the hiking trail itself.

"And sometimes when you'd get up in the middle of the night you'd hear the reassuring thump, thump of her tail on the floor, letting you know that she was there and thinking of you."
- William Cole

The Best of the Best...

The 10 Best Places To Hike With Your Dog In The Reno/Lake Tahoe Area

(Blue Ribbon)   Rancho San Rafael Park (city of Reno)

A Reno showcase, beautifully landscaped Rancho San Rafael Park serves up several enticing canine hikes: a self-guided nature trail through the many plant zones of the Great Basin, a gravel footpath that circles the wide open spaces of the park, and access to the trails of Peavine Mountain. This park is a favorite for exercising your dog.

(#2)   Virginia Lake (city of Reno)

This quiet 21-acre park feels much as it must have when it was founded more than 60 years ago. Little has been altered around the edges of Virginia Lake. One thing that has changed - to the delight of dog owners - is a fenced-in, off-leash dogpark at the northern end of the park.

(#3)   Sparks Marina Park (city of Sparks)

The conversion of an abandoned quarry into a popular lake has earned the City of Sparks national recognition. A concrete walking path surrounds the Sparks marina and covers almost two miles. The trail system is lighted for evening walks with the dog. The dogpark is the only off-leash dogpark in the Reno area for dogs to play in the water.

(#4)   Mount Rose Wilderness (Lake Tahoe - North Shore)

Even if you decide not to complete the 6-mile, 2000-foot ascent to the summit of Mount Rose, there is plenty here to thrill canine hikers. More than 20 miles of designated trails are available through the canyons and ridges of the high country of the Carson Range. This is the closest wilderness area to Reno.

(#5)   Prey Meadows/Skunk Harbor (Lake Tahoe - East Shore)

One of the prettiest canine hikes in Lake Tahoe is the 1.5-mile trek to Prey Meadows and Skunk Harbor. Stroll through thick pines to the meadow, stealing glimpses of the lake as you go. Skunk Harbor is a charming cove with a sandy beach. Beside the path lie remains of an old railroad built in the 1870s to haul timber from Lake Tahoe to Virginia City.

(#6)   Galena Creek Park (city of Reno)

Any level of canine hiker can enjoy 440-acre Galena Creek Park, which once housed a fish hatchery supplying trout to Northern Nevada. An easy, self-guided Nature Trail navigates through the park's rich forests - pause to breathe in the rich vanilla fragrance of the Ponderosa pines. More demanding trails climb into the eastern slopes of the Sierra Nevadas.

(#7)   Caughlin Ranch (city of Reno)

This planned residential community maintains a 36-mile network of parks and trails the public is welcome to explore. Even though the hikes are often right along the road, the trails still feel like an escape into nature. Your dog can often sniff rabbits, ducks and other wildlife along these paved paths.

(#8)   Davis Creek Park (city of Carson City)

Davis Creek offers miles of hiking trails, including routes to Price Lake and the Tahoe Meadows on Mount Rose. Less ambitious canine hikers will enjoy the half-mile nature trail around a tiny pond. The Discovery Trail around the park perimeter is another paw-friendly trail. The spectacular pine trees in Davis Creek Park are some of the oldest in the Tahoe area, survivors of the clear-cutting of the 19th century because they were on private land.

(#9)   Hawley Grade National Recreation Trail (Lake Tahoe - East Shore)

The old road connecting Echo Summit to the Upper Lake Valley was built by Asa Hawley in 1855. It was the first wagon road into the Tahoe Basin. Today your dog can trot along this historic path.

(#10)   Pyramid Lake (Sutcliffe)

All the fun at Nevada's largest natural lake isn't on the water. There are sandy trails along the shoreline of the 30-mile lake and rocky paths on the eastern flank that lead to interesting tufa formations of blanched white rock. There isn't much shade around the water in the summer but Pyramid Lake makes a great canine swimming hole.

The 10 Best Trails To Hike With Your Dog In The Reno/Lake Tahoe Region For Less Than One Hour

There are many great places to walk your dog around Reno and Lake Tahoe. But what if you only had one hour to walk one trail with your dog, where would you go? Here are ten candidates for the perfect dog walking experience on a time budget:

🐾 **Bartley Ranch**
Your dog will find the two miles of sandy hiking trails on this former working ranch expecially paw-friendly.

🐾 **Cascade Creek Falls**
This one-mile linear trail travels through a shady fir forest on the way to thundering 200-foot Cascade Creek Falls.

🐾 **Dayton State Park**
The Carson River Trail makes for a superior canine hike - flat and sandy, in the shade of mature cotton-woods, with grand views of the water and the 150-year old town of Dayton.

🐾 **Idlewild Park**
A dogwalking tour of this traditional downtown park on the banks of the Truckee River will include looks at the Mission-style architecture of the California Building and the natural beauty of the Rose Garden.

🐾 **Prey Meadows/Skunk Harbor**
This short Lake Tahoe hike is treasured for its beauty, from springtime wildflower displays to the pale green sagebrush that grows in only a few parts of the lake.

🐾 **Rancho San Rafael Park**
Try the paw-friendly one-mile nature trail for an introduction to the unique plants of the Great Basin.

Stateline Lookout
It is a scant half-mile hike to the free telescopes at Stateline Lookout that offer incomparable views of Lake Tahoe.

Taylor Creek Visitors Center
You have your choice of short hikes here. Everyone will want to experience the Stream Profile Chamber Trail with its cut-away underwater views of Taylor Creek. Don't miss the newly renovated Rainbow Trail that explains the importance of marshes and meadows to the crystal clarity of Lake Tahoe.

Verdi Nature Study Park
This packed sand trail is scarcely 1/2 mile long but that is far enough to pass through sagebrush flats edged with large black pines and even the remains of an old logging flume.

Virginia Lake
A one-mile path circles the lake and is easy walking the entire way, with only a small rise waiting at the southern end of the trail.

I can't think of anything that brings me closer to tears than when my old dog - completely exhausted after a hard day in the field - limps away from her nice spot in front of the fire and comes over to where I'm sitting and puts her head in my lap, a paw over my knee, and closes her eyes, and goes back to sleep. I don't know what I've done to deserve that kind of friend."
-Gene Hill

10 Cool Things To See On Reno/Lake Tahoe Trails With Your Dog

"If your dog is fat," the old saying goes, "you aren't getting enough exercise." But walking the dog need not be just about a little exercise. Here are 10 cool things you can see around Reno and Lake Tahoe while out walking the dog.

Colorful Fish

Walking the dog down the Stream Profile Chamber Trail at Taylor Creek Visitors Center leads to a cut-away view of the creek and its underwater denizens. In fall, spawning Kokanee salmon, tinted a brilliant red, swim past the window (your dog will have to wait outside however). Another place to view colorful fish up close is on the Truckee River Bike Path in Tahoe City. Peer into the water off the side of Fanny Bridge and look at rainbow trout in the headwaters of the Truckee.

Famous Roads

In the mid-1800s the Reno area was merely a stopover on the way to somewhere else. Many roads were used by wagon trains, the Pony Express and others to reach California including Hawley's Grade, the detour through Dog Valley and mountain passes such as Roller Pass, Donner Pass and Carson Pass. Today, many of these historic routes are public trails hosting canine hikers. Keep an eye out for faint rust marks on rocks that are souvenirs of the wagon wheels of the western migration.

Geology

The geologic origins of the region reveal themselves in many spots along local trails. At Cascade Creek Falls ridges on both sides of Cascade Lake are visible where rock debris has been pushed by retreating glaciers. This depression, like other similar pits scraped from the rock, filled with snow melt and rainwater to form Tahoe area lakes.

🐾 Gravestones

Cemeteries are good destinations for an off-beat canine hike. In Virginia City, the nation's largest federally maintained historic district, are separate cemeteries reminiscent of the boomtown's rigidly structured society. Wander among the headstones that are markers from a time when Virginia City was Nevada's biggest town.

🐾 Historic Buildings

Area parks are home to some of Reno/Lake Tahoe's most historic buildings. Relocated to Bartley Ranch is the one-room Huffaker School that predates even Reno itself. In Idlewild Park stands the California Building, built in 1927 and now the home of the Reno Art Center. From that same era, near the Loch Levens Lake trailhead, is the Rainbow Lodge, constructed from hand-hewn logs. Even older, dating back a century, are rustic farm buildings seen from the trails of Wilson Commons Park.

🐾 Interesting Boulders

The Reno/Lake Tahoe region is rife with souvenirs from its glaciated past. Many of these boulders were used by Washo Indians to grind food - look for smoothed depressions in the granite rocks as an indication it may have been a grinding boulder. One good place to see these stones, and learn their story, is at the Lam Watah Washo Heritage Site. Pyramid Lake was named for a triangular-shaped rock that can be seen from trails along its southern shore. And canine hikers on Peavine Mountain can visit the boulders that University of Nevada students first arranged into a symbolic "N" in 1913. The stones are still maintained today.

Magnificent Estates

Your dog can walk up close and marvel at three estates at the Tallac Historic Site - the Pope Estate, the Heller Estate and the Baldwin Estate. Wooded footpaths connect the mansion sites. You can see, but not visit with your dog, Vikingsholm in Lake Tahoe at Eagle Falls and Bower's Mansion at Davis Creek State Park.

Old Fort Ruins

Fort Churchill State Park contains the ruins of the 1861 frontier fort built to secure overland migration routes. Fort Churchill lasted only a decade and has been in a state of arrested decay ever since. The remains of the adobe buildings can be seen from trails in the state park.

TV and Movie Locations

Your dog can walk in the footsteps of famous Hollywood actors at sites in the Reno/Lake Tahoe region used to film television shows and movies. The Lower Prey Meadows on Tahoe's eastern shore was a prime location for establishing shots of the great NBC western, "Bonanza." Hoss, Little Joe, Adam and Ben Cartwright could often be seen riding through this lush meadow in the shadow of towering mountains. Any canine hike to Dayton State Park will bring you in the vicinity of filming locations for *The Misfits*, Clark Gable and Marilyn Monroe's last movie.

Waterfalls

The Reno/Lake Tahoe region is certainly not lacking in picturesque waterfalls you can visit with your dog. Some, like Heath Falls, ask for considerable trail time but others like Cascade Creek Falls and Eagle Falls, the only waterfall emptying directly into Lake Tahoe, can be enjoyed with very little purchase.

"No animal should ever jump up on the dining room furniture unless...he can hold his own in the conversation."
       -Fran Liebowitz

The 40 Best Places To Hike With Your Dog In The Reno/Lake Tahoe Region

1
Rancho San Rafael Park

The Park

A natural wonder in the middle of Reno, Rancho San Rafael Park is new compared to many other parks in the area; it opened in 1982. A gift to the city by entrepreneur and department store magnate Wilbur D. May, the park features the May museum and arboretum, as well as picnic areas, and the restored ranch house (a favorite for weddings and special gatherings). Every September the park plays host to the Great Reno Balloon Races. Scores

Reno

Distance from downtown Reno
- less than 2 miles
Phone Number
- (775) 785-4319
Website
- www.washoecountyparks.com/ parks/pk_detail.asp?PkId=5
Admission Fee
- None
Directions
- From downtown, travel north on Virginia Street to 9th Street. Turn left on 9th, and travel one block to Sierra Street. Turn right on Sierra, and travel 1.5 miles north to the park. The entrance is next to a concrete entrance arch on the left. Parking is plentiful throughout the park.

of hot air balloons fill the early morning skies over Reno with a kaleidoscope of colors and shapes. During the festival balloons launch from Rancho San Rafael every morning for three days, engage in special races, and land throughout the city.

The Walks

The trails of beautifully landscaped Rancho San Rafael Park are an excellent place to experience the high desert of the Great Basin, one of the most unusual and diverse habitats in the United States. Elevations soar to over 10,000 feet from hundreds of feet below sea level, and varied environmental zones range from alpine to desert. The one-mile, self-guided nature trail provides a pleasant, easy walk along a sandy path

34

that introduces some of the unique plants growing in the Great Basin. A gravel hiking and walking path circles the perimeter of the wide open park, and is a favorite of runners and their dogs. Across McCarran Boulevard, the park continues at the base of Peavine Mountain. Many trails branch off the main stem of this hike, that steepens in its last paces. Although cottonwoods shade the developed areas of Rancho San Rafael, most of the hiking here is under the sun.

Dog Friendliness

Dogs on leash are welcome on all trails, but not on maintained turf areas in the park, or in the May Arboretum. Take a break from the trail, and play a game of Frisbee with your dog in the large, non-maintained grassy area near McCarran Boulevard. Dogs can be seen romping on this large expanse of open ground most times of the day.

Traffic

Rancho San Rafael is a roomy park - you rarely run into large groups of dogwalkers. Early in the morning is one of the best times to enjoy the park; many people begin their day with a walk or run with their dog alongside.

Canine Swimming

Dogs are welcome to swim in the creek areas when there is water available.

Trail Time

Fifteen minutes to more than an hour.

2

Virginia Lake

The Park

Roger Teglia, pioneer Reno rancher and founder of the Nevada Fish & Game Association in 1932, was instrumental in getting this land for the city. Construction on the park began during the Depression as a public works project and was completed in 1939. Original stonework can still be seen at the northwest end of the lake. The now-dry fountain on the eastern side of the lake is a remnant of that time as well. Today the sylvan qualities of Virginia Lake are much as they were in 1939 - no concessions, no boats and no future plans to mar the peace and quiet of the the lake and 22-acre park.

Reno

Distance from downtown Reno
- less than 2 miles
Phone Number
- (775) 334-2262
Website
- www.cityofreno.com/
com_service /parks/
dogparks.html
Admission Fee
- None
Directions
- From downtown Reno take Virginia Street south to Plumb Lane. Turn right on Plumb and follow one block to Lakeside. Turn left, continuing right on Lakeside one block further south. The drive circles the park.

The Walks

A paved one-mile path loops around the edge of Virginia Lake with its blue waters and new floating fountains. The path is easy walking, with only a small climb waiting at the southern end of the trail. The route winds among shade trees, ducks and geese.

Roger Teglia is also remembered at Teglia's Paradise Park on the border of Reno and Sparks, just off Oddie Boulevard. The City of Reno renovated the once neglected wetlands here in 1998 and created a thriving pond stocked with trout and visited by many species of birds including gulls, ducks and Canadian geese. A one-mile packed dirt trails circles this pond as well.

Dog Friendliness
Leashed dogs are welcome at Virginia Lake.

Traffic
This is Reno's most popular park, busy at all times of day with joggers, strollers and other dog walkers.

Canine Swimming
Dogs are not allowed in Virginia Lake.

Trail Time
Less than an hour.

"They are superior to human beings as companions. They do not quarrel or argue with you. They never talk about themselves but listen to you while you talk about yourself, and keep an appearance of being interested in the conversation."

- Jerome K. Jerome

3

Sparks Marina Park

The Park

For more than a century beginning in 1861, this area was the Nichols Ranch. The land was sold in 1967 to the Helms Construction Company who quarried out gravel and dirt for the next 25 years, excavating nearly 10,000,000 cubic yards of aggregate before going out of business in 1992. The City of Sparks was then awarded the land for public use and benefit.

The City planned to create a lake in the abandoned pit and estimated it would take three years to fill the quarry with water. As it happened, the job would take less than three days. Heavy snowmelt and rains conspired to trigger record floods in the Truckee River Basin on New Year's Day of 1997 and one billion gallons of water poured into the quarry to depths greater than 100 feet.

The Sparks Public Works Department set about stabilizing the walls of the new lake and grading the surrounding land. Sparks Marina Park was dedicated on October 5, 2000 and in 2002 was named the National Public Works Project of the Year.

Sparks

Distance from downtown Reno
- 5 1/2 miles
Phone Number
- (775) 353-2376
Website
- www.ci.sparks.nv.us/
redevelopment/marina/
Admission Fee
- None
Directions
- Take Virginia Street to Interstate 80, and head east to McCarran Boulevard. Turn left at the bottom of the off ramp, and follow McCarran to Lincoln Way. Turn right on Lincoln Way, and follow to Howard. You will see the park ahead of you. Park in one of several lots surrounding the park.

The Walks

Sparks Marina Park features a 1.8-mile wide, concrete path that traces the shore of the entire marina. Views across the lake extend to Reno and the Sierra Nevada beyond. The trail system is lighted so you can catch an evening walk with the dog.

Dog Friendliness

A highlight of Sparks Marina Park is a dog park on the south side of the marina. The park features a dog-level drinking fountain and a bright red community fire hydrant. Dogs are allowed throughout the park except on the human beach.

Traffic

This new Sparks park is a hub of activity during the summer, especially on weekends. Winter dog-walking is a more solitary affair.

Canine Swimming

The dog park, with its sandy beach and 150 feet of lakeshore, is the only off-leash dog park in the Reno area for dogs to play in the water. The marina is a delight for the nautically-inclined dog. In addition to swimming, other human activities include sailing, scuba diving and fishing.

Trail Time

Less than an hour.

"Any man who does not like dogs and want them does not deserve to be in the White House."
- Calvin Coolidge

4

Mount Rose Wilderness

The Park

Mount Rose Wilderness, including 10,776-foot Mount Rose and Mount Rose Meadows, was created in 1989. It is the closest wilderness area to Reno. Three major Northern Nevada ski areas operate within a short distance of Mount Rose and in winter cross-country skiers are always out enjoying the meadow trails.

The Walks

More than 20 miles of designated canine hiking on four major trails pierce this 28,000-acre wilderness area. The marquee trail is the 6-mile, 2,000-foot ascent to the summit of Mount Rose. Your reward is magnificent views of Lake Tahoe, Truckee Meadows and, on clear days, Pyramid Lake. Although much of the trail is paw-friendly hard-packed sand, the last two miles on the ridge traverse rough shale and give sharp, uncertain footing to a dog. Other trails exploring the canyons and ridges of the high country of the Carson Range include the 8-mile Jones/Whites Creek loop trail and, in the northern section of the wilderness, the 2-mile Hunter Creek trail. The 3-mile Thomas Creek trail leads canine hikers to small lakes and active meadows in the interior of the park.

Lake Tahoe/North Shore

Distance from downtown Reno
  - 26 miles
Phone Number
  - (775) 832-4107
Website
  - www.cdnp.org
Admission Fee
  - None
Directions
  - Take Virginia Street to Interstate 80 East to Highway 395. Follow Highway 395 south to the Mount Rose Interchange. Bear right at the Interchange onto State Highway 431, the Mount Rose Highway. Follow the Mount Rose Highway almost to the summit of Mount Rose (8,933 feet), about 15 miles. The parking area for the trailheads will be on your left, in the Mount Rose Meadows.

Dog Friendliness

Dogs are welcome on the trails in the wilderness area.

Traffic

Mount Rose Wilderness is Nevada's most heavily-used wilderness area. The Mount Rose Trail is extremely popular - as many as 200 hikers on a weekend day can be encountered going up and down the mountain. Try one of the lower trails if the parking lot is full. Bikes and horses are not allowed on the paved Mount Rose Meadows trail.

Canine Swimming

Creeks and ponds are available for doggie-paddling.

Trail Time

More than an hour.

5

Prey Meadows / Skunk Harbor

The Park

For centuries towering stands of Ponderosa pines grew unmolested on the dark green slopes of Lake Tahoe. Then silver was discovered in Virginia City in the mid-1800s. Lumber was needed in a hurry to construct the boomtown and axes began flying around the lakeshore. When things settled down, the first public lands in the Lake Tahoe Basin were established in 1899 as the Lake Tahoe Forest Reserve totaling 37,000 acres - but with no lakefront property. Today, 25% of the 72-mile shoreline and 158,500 acres in the Basin are federally owned.

Lake Tahoe/East Shore

Distance from downtown Reno
- 40 miles
Phone Number
- (530) 573-2600
Website
- www.r5.fs.fed.us/ltbmu/visitor/hiking/north&east.htm.
Admission Fee
- None
Directions
- Take Virginia Street to Interstate 80 East to Highway 395 and go south towards Carson City. Follow Highway 395 to the Mount Rose Interchange and bear right onto Highway 431, the Mount Rose Highway until it ends at Highway 28. Turn left, toward Incline Village, continuing past Sand Harbor to the iron pipe gate on the right side of the highway, about 6 miles past the Ponderosa Ranch. Park in turnouts along the highway, making sure not to block the gate.

The Walks

One of the prettiest canine hikes in Lake Tahoe is the 1.5-mile trek to Prey Meadows and Skunk Harbor, two lovely ornaments on the east shore of Lake Tahoe. Filtered views of the lake peek through the thick pines as you wander along an easy flat access road. Beside the path rest the remains of an old railroad grade built in the 1870s as part of the network of rail lines and flumes that supplied timber to Virginia City. The main path forks after a short walk. The left fork leads to

Prey Meadows, treasured for its springtime wildflower displays and views of the pale green sagebrush that grows in only a few parts of the lake. The right fork winds towards Skunk Harbor, a charming cove with a sandy beach.

Dog Friendliness

Dogs are welcome on the trails here.

Traffic

This trail gets plenty of foot traffic in the summertime but is generally only moderately used.

Canine Swimming

This is one of the best area spots for canine aquatics with easy access to Lake Tahoe.

Trail Time

Less than an hour.

"The greatest pleasure of a dog is that you may make a fool of yourself with him, and not only will he not scold you, but will make a fool of himself too."
- Samuel Butler

6

Galena Creek Park

The Park

Galena Creek, like many areas around Reno and Lake Tahoe, began life as a mining community. The original town of Galena was located in the Callahan Road area about five miles down the Mount Rose Highway. An early ski resort bounded the area in the 1930s and Galena Park was used mainly for picnicking. Today, the 440-acre park, which once housed a fish hatchery supplying trout to Northern Nevada, is a recreation destination year round, hosting sledders and cross-country skiers in the winter.

Reno

Distance from downtown Reno
  - 18 miles
Phone Number
  - (775) 849-2511
Website
  - www.washoecountyparks.com/ parks/pk_detail.asp?PkId=4
Admission Fee
  - None
Directions
  - From downtown Reno take Interstate 80 East to Highway 395 and on south towards Carson City. Continue about 10 miles to the Mount Rose exit, and bear to the right with the highway to travel up Mount Rose. The park is seven miles up Highway 431, the Mount Rose Highway, on the right.

The Walks

Many trails crisscross Galena Creek Park, including the self-guiding Nature Trail that is an easy affair for any level of canine hiker. Numerous songbirds call the park home, along with a noisy pack of Stellar's jays and golden-mantled ground squirrels who will welcome a stray dog treat from your pocket. Snuggled in a delightful forest along the base of Mount Rose, Galena Creek is filled with Ponderosa and Jeffrey pines, and, closer to the creek, alder, aspen and dogwood. Pause for a breath as you hike and take in the rich vanilla fragrance of the Ponderosa pines - easily identified by their rough, reddish bark.

More demanding trails climb the eastern slope of the SierraNevada along the park's meandering creeks and into the Mount Rose Wilderness Area. The popular Jones Creek Trail is a 9.5-mile loop that traces Jones Creek and White's Creek through conifer forests, up canyons and across ridges. The trail gains altitude for at least two miles and canine hikers will find the right loop a more moderate climb. The creeks often flood with heavy rainfall and during the spring melt so check with rangers for updates on trail damage before heading out.

Dog Friendliness

Dogs are welcome on the hiking trails at Galena Creek Park.

Traffic

Trails within park boundaries are for foot traffic, including equestrians, only. Use of the park - one of the most beautiful close to Reno - is heavy summer or winter.

Canine Swimming

Dog paddling is a summer treat in Church's Pond, if you take the longer hike, and there is splashing aplenty in Jones, Galena and White's creeks.

Trail Time

More than an hour.

7

Caughlin Ranch

The Park

For many decades Caughlin Ranch (pronounced "Cawlin") was a productive cattle ranch. In 1984 developers began converting 2300 acres of land into a planned community of more than 3000 homes. Fully half of Caughlin Ranch - 1150 acres - was kept as natural open space and the development is characterized by a park-like setting with native plants, landscaping and ponds. The family ranch house is now restored and a proud part of Crissie Caughlin Park on Mayberry Drive in Reno.

Reno

Distance from downtown Reno
 - 4 miles
Phone Number
 - None
Website
 - None
Admission Fee
 - None
Directions
 - Take Virginia Street to Interstate 80, and take Interstate 80 west to McCarran Boulevard. Head west off the ramp. Turn left on McCarran, and follow to Caughlin Parkway. Turn right on Caughlin Parkway, and follow to the beginning of the asphalt trail, which will be on your right.

The Walks

Caughlin Ranch features a 36-mile network of parks and trails the public is welcome to explore. The paths are wide and paved (good to keep those canine nails short). One route popular with dog walkers begins just west of McCarran Boulevard on Caughlin Parkway. It meanders upwards until ending at the Eagles Nest subdivision. Along the serpentine path, canine hikers will find numerous duck ponds where dogs can pause to enjoy a cool drink. Even though much of the trail is right along the road, it seems miles away from the noise and hurry of everyday life. Your dog can often sniff rabbits, ducks, and other wildlife along this trail.

Dog Friendliness

Dogs from outside the neighborhood are welcome on the trails of this private community. Some folks, however, are discouraging use of the trail as it passes their property so people and dogs may find access blocked in spots.

Traffic

Dogs will see everything on wheels from strollers to bikes to rollerbladers along these paved paths.

Canine Swimming

Dogs are not allowed to swim in the ponds.

Trail Time

Less than an hour to several hours.

8

Davis Creek Park

The Park

Davis Creek Park, in the thickly forested Washoe Valley at the base of the Carson Range, was originally a part of the Winters Ranch. The rambling old ranch house and outbuildings near the intersection of Highway 395 and Nevada 429 are the only surviving buildings of the Winters spread. The pond in the group picnic area is also a remant of the land's ranching days but the most important souvenir from that time in Davis Creek Park is a large stand of Jeffrey Pines. These trees - some of the oldest timber in the area - survived cutting to support the Virginia City mines only because they were on private land. Washoe County opened Davis Creek Park in 1968.

Carson City

Distance from downtown Reno
- 21 miles
Phone Number
- (775) 849-0684
Website
- www.washoecountyparks.com/
parks/pk_detail.asp?PkId=3
Admission Fee
- None
Directions
- From downtown Reno take Interstate 80 East to the Highway 395 offramp. Head south, towards Carson City. Follow Highway 395 South to Exit 57B- towards Virginia City/Carson City/Lake Tahoe. Continue on Highway 395 to Nevada 429 and turn right. Follow Route 429 to the park, which is on the left.

The Walks

Davis Creek offers miles and miles of hiking trails, including the Ophir Creek Trail, which climbs to Price Lake and the Tahoe Meadows on Mount Rose. It also hooks up with the Tahoe Rim Trail and trails in the Mount Rose Wilderness. The route is very rough and rocky, and not for the inexperienced hiking paw. Better choices for canine hikers are two trails closer to the valley floor. The half-mile Nature Trail circles the three-acre pond and is a flat and sandy walk. A brochure and trailside markers detail plant life thriving in the lush surroundings. Similarly, the Discovery Trail tours the perimeter of the park for 1.5 miles.

Dog Friendliness

Dogs are welcome throughout Davis Creek Park.

Traffic

There is stiff competition for the trails on weekends but weekday canine hikers can often enjoy a virtually empty park.

Canine Swimming

Dogs are allowed to swim in the pond but during dry years the water can be brackish and stale.

Trail Time

More than an hour.

"A door is what a dog is perpetually on the wrong side of."
                                    - James Thurber

9

Hawley Grade National Recreation Trail

The Park

Asa Hawley built the first wagon road into the Tahoe Basin in 1855, connecting Echo Summit to upper Lake Valley. The road served as a vital link between Placerville, California and Genoa, Nevada and business boomed along the trail after silver was discovered in Virginia City in 1859. Plans were already underway for a transcontinental railroad, however, and when the line was completed in 1869 traffic on the road went into steep decline. When US 50, "America's Main Street," opened in the 1920s the old Hawley Road was doomed to extinction.

The Walks

The trek up the Hawley Grade is steady going but not overly steep or difficult for any dog. The trail starts in a large stand of aspen and is flat and sandy. Remnants of past travelers begin to infest the landscape - an old wooden water tank is nestled between two large granite boulders and a stone cistern overlooks the trail. The Hawley Grade National Recreation Trail is an out-and-back affair covering 3.5 miles round

Lake Tahoe - East Shore
Distance from downtown Reno   - 21 miles
Phone Number   - (775) 849-0684

Website
  - www.washoecountyparks.com/
  parks/pk_detail.asp?PkId=3

Admission Fee   - None
Directions   - Take Virginia Street to Interstate 80, and go east to Highway 395 south towards Carson City. Follow Highway 395 through the Mount Rose Interchange following the signs to Carson City. Continue through Carson City, to US 50 on the south end of Carson City. Turn right on US 50, and continue through South Lake Tahoe to the "Y," where US 50 merges with Highway 89. Turn left on US 50 and follow south for 5.3 miles, then turn left onto the South Upper Truckee Road. The road narrows to one lane about 3 miles into the drive. Follow 3.8 miles and turn at the Hawley Grade sign. Continue .3 mile more to the end of the road and park your car in the area off the road.

trip. Gorgeous pines, a deciduous forest and views of Lake
Tahoe flavor your dog-walk through history here.

Dog Friendliness

Dogs are welcome up and down the Hawley Grade.

Traffic

Expect to share the old road with mountain bikes and
some sections can be narrow, rocky and travel over pure rock.

Canine Swimming

Dogs can find some canine swimming in the Upper Truckee
River and there are some small water holes along a short loop
at the beginning of the hike.

Trail Time

More than an hour.

10
Pyramid Lake

The Park

Human habitation along these shores dates back 11,000 years when nomadic Paiute tribes camped here. Explorer John Fremont wrote in his journal about his discovery of Nevada's largest natural lake in 1844: ". . . we continued our way up the hollow, intending to see what lay beyond the mountain. The hollow was several miles long, forming a good pass; the snow deepening to about a foot as we neared the summit. Beyond, a defile between the mountains descended rapidly about two thousand feet; and, filling up all the lower space, was a sheet of green water, some twenty miles broad. It broke upon our eyes like the ocean." Fremont named the lake for the large pyramid-shaped rock jutting from the water near the south shore. The Paiute elders negotiated a reservation treaty for the rights to Pyramid Lake in 1874 but it didn't stop the land grab around the lake. Today Pyramid Lake lies entirely within the Paiute Reservation.

Sutcliffe

Distance from downtown Reno
- 40 miles
Phone Number
- (775) 574-1155
Website
- www.plpt.nsn.us/
Admission Fee
- Permit required for all non-tribal members
Directions
- Take Virginia Street to Interstate 80, and Interstate 80 east to Pyramid Highway (Nevada 445). Follow Pyramid Highway north to Pyramid Lake, about 40 miles. Turn left and follow Nevada 446 to the town of Sutcliffe.

The Walks

There are trails throughout the Pyramid Lake area, which is mostly sagebrush and sandstone. There are sandy trails along the shoreline of the 30-mile long lake and rocky paths on the eastern flank that lead to interesting tufa forma-

tions of bleached white rock. Shady breaks for the dog in
summer are few.

Dog Friendliness

Dogs are welcome on the Reservation. Some areas, including the Needles at the north end of the lake, are off-limits to
visitors, with or without a dog.

Traffic

Empty beaches and trails are the rule at Pyramid Lake.

Canine Swimming

Pyramid Lake is one giant canine swimming hole, but
beware of ledges that drop off not far from the beaches.

Trail Time

More than an hour.

11

Tallac Historic Site

The Park

Several buildings from three separate estates make up the Tallac Historic Site. They were all built on the lake from the 1890s through the 1920s. The Pope Estate included a man-made trout pond with a cascading waterfall, and a fully stocked arboretum. The Heller Estate included the "Valhalla" building, which is used today for community and private events during nine months of the year. The Baldwin Estate belonged to Lucky Baldwin, a wealthy California real estate investor and entrepreneur, and included a courtyard with a wishing well, a hotel, and a casino. The Forest Service acquired the area between 1969 and 1971, and has been restoring and renovating ever since.

Lake Tahoe - South Shore

Distance from downtown Reno
- 60 miles
Phone Number
- (530) 542-4166
Website
- www.valhalla-tallac.com/
Admission Fee
- None
Directions
- Take Virginia Street to Interstate 80 east to Highway 395 south towards Carson City. Follow Highway 395 through the Mount Rose Interchange following the signs to Carson City. Continue through Carson City, to US 50 on the south end of Carson City. Turn right on US 50, and continue through South Lake Tahoe to the "Y," where US 50 merges with Highway 89. Turn right on Highway 89, and follow north about 3.5 miles to the entrance on your right. The entrance and parking areas are on the lake side of the highway.

The Walks

A large paved path runs through the Pope and Baldwin estates for about .75 miles, connecting fragant pine forests on both homesites. It is flat and an easy trot for any dog. Along the trail is a wayside exhibit on the Washo Indians who summered on these Lake Tahoe shores.

Dog Friendliness

Dogs aren't allowed inside the museums but are welcome to trot the trails.

Traffic

The pine forests between the estates can be a place to seek refuge from summer tourist crowds.

Canine Swimming

The Tallac Historic Site offers no canine swimming but Kiva Beach will set tails wagging on water-loving dogs.

Trail Time

You can spend hours wandering the trails and visiting the magnificent estates here.

12

Lake Tahoe State Park

The Park

This land for centuries was the summering ground of the Washoe Indians. When logging companies arrived in the 1860s to harvest timber for the Comstock Lode silver rush, they stripped the area completely of trees. All the growth you see today is reforested second growth. Lake Tahoe State Park encompasses 14,000 acres, over 12,000 of which are backcountry wilderness.

The Walks

Lake Tahoe State Park offers something for every level of canine hiker. An interpretive trail circumnavigates Spooner Lake, named for the Canadian-born timber baron Michele E. Spooner. This flat dirt trail is easy walking for 1 3/4 miles through aspen groves and meadows spiced with views of the lake and surrounding area. Signs explain the diverse plant and animal life that inhabit the area - look for bald eagles and ospreys. For more rigorous canine hikes, hook into the spectacular Tahoe Rim Trail.

Lake Tahoe - East Shore

Distance from downtown Reno
- 50 miles
Phone Number
- (775) 831-0494
Website
- www.state.nv.us/stparks/lt.htm
Admission Fee
- Yes
Directions
- Take Virginia Street to Interstate 80; go east to Highway 395 and south to Carson City, through Mount Rose Interchange, following the signs to Carson City. Continue through town to the US 50 Lake Tahoe turnoff, which is past Carson City on the right.
Turn right, and follow US 50 up the mountain to Spooner Lake, about 9 miles. Turn right on Highway 28 and follow a few hundred feet to the park entrance, which is on the right.

And in winter, Spooner Lake Meadows is a great place for your dog when you take to cross-country skis. Lake Tahoe State Park maintains more than 60 miles of groomed cross-country ski trails.

Dog Friendliness
Dogs are permitted on the trails but not at Sand Harbor.

Traffic
This park is extremely popular with mountain bikers and they are banned from some trails completely and others on odd days. If you want to avoid them, check the posted schedules.

Canine Swimming
Spooner Lake is an excellent place for dogs to show off their dog paddling strokes.

Trail Time
More than an hour.

"Money will buy a pretty good dog
but it won't buy the wag of his tail."
- Josh Billings

13

Truckee River Walk

The Park

The name Truckee comes to the 21st century from a friendly Paiute Indian guide who assisted thousand of emigrants across the Humboldt Sink. His name was thought to sound like "tro-key." This walking path, developed to highlight the Truckee River, extends from Sparks through Reno, and beyond. Developed in the 1980s, the pathway is dedicated to Raymond Smith, founder of Harold's Club. His casino on Virginia Street brought Reno's gaming industry out of the backrooms and dusky halls. The River Walk portion of the path in downtown Reno passes through the heart of the city's redevelopment project.

Reno/Sparks

Distance from downtown Reno
- in town
Phone Number
- (775) 329-6008
Website
- None
Admission Fee
- None
Directions
- From downtown Reno take Virginia Street to First Street. You'll see the Truckee River as it winds through Reno. The path runs along both sides of the river here. Follow it west and you'll pass through Arlington Park, Idlewild Park, and on toward West Fourth Street and Verdi. Follow it east and you'll pass by the Reno Hilton and into Sparks and Fisherman's Park.

The Walks

Much of the main trail is paved with sandy dirt spurs and short, rocky paths leading to the Truckee River. Access to the path is plentiful throughout Reno and Sparks - you can walk through the bustle of downtown Reno and still see cormorants, gulls and ducks bobbing in the river. Canine hikers can also track the trail into less developed areas and feel miles away from the city you have left only minutes behind. A favorite stop along the River Walk for canine hikers in Sparks is landscaped Rock Park with plenty of open lawn areas, shady trees and bushes.

Dog Friendliness

Dogs are welcome to join in the fun along the Truckee River Walk.

Traffic

This a popular trail through heavily populated areas. Dog walkers will be dodging bicycles, rollerblades and street traffic.

Canine Swimming

The Truckee River is frequently available for water-loving dogs on this path. In many places the river rushes through boulders and dangerous currents, so beware.

Trail Time

Any length of dog walking experience can be sculpted from the Truckee River Walk.

14

Fallen Leaf Lake

The Park

Nathan Gilmore, a farmer from Ohio, was one of the first to exploit the beauty of this area. In 1873 he began bottling and selling mineral water, tinted brown from its high iron content, obtained at Glen Alpine Creek, the major feeder source for Fallen Leaf Lake. He soon built Soda Springs resort, courting the rich and famous. The spa was abandoned in 1967 with several buildings already collapsing. The Forest Service acquired the land in 1977 and the nine remaining resort buildings from Glen Alpine Springs, unrestored all, still stand as silent testament to a bygone era.

Lake Tahoe - South Shore

Distance from downtown Reno
 - 65 miles
Phone Number
 - (530) 573-2674
Website
 - www.r5.fs.fed.us/ltbmu/visitor
Admission Fee
 - Permit required for wilderness hiking
Directions
 - Take Virginia Street to Interstate 80 east to Highway 395 and south towards Carson City. Follow Highway 395 through the Mount Rose Interchange following the signs to Carson City. Continue through Carson City, to US 50 on the south end of Carson City. Turn right on US 50, and continue through South Lake Tahoe to the "Y," where US 50 merges with Highway 89. Turn right on Highway 89, and follow about 3 miles to Fallen Leaf Lake Road. Turn left, and follow about 1 mile to the parking lot near the campground entrance.

The Walks

Fallen Leaf Lake, the largest of the satellite lakes around Lake Tahoe, can keep a canine hiker delighted for weeks. There are many trails in the area, including gateways to the hundreds of miles of backcountry hiking in the Desolation Wilderness, the most heavily used wilderness area in the United States. One of the most popular walks kicks off near the entance of the campground and can be as short as 3/4 of a mile or as

60

long as two miles. After a small rise, the route drops down to the rocky shore and a fine wide trail continues through fragrant pine forests around the lake or along Taylor Creek. Another favorite is the hike to Glen Alpine Falls, an easy one-mile roundtrip to breathtaking views of the tumbling waters. The Upper Falls, wide and powerful, drop 30 feet before finishing their plunge with a 75-foot cascade down the step-like Lower Falls. Continue another mile up the trail to view the remains of Glen Alpine Springs resort.

Dog Friendliness

Dogs are welcome on the trails around Fallen Leaf Lake.

Traffic

These trails, especially the short walks to popular landmarks, are crowded in the summer but thin out in the off-season.

Canine Swimming

There are plenty of opportunities for your dog to get in a good swim, in either Glen Alpine Creek or Fallen Leaf Lake, but the water may be COLD!

Trail Time

From less than an hour to days if you head into the Desolation Wilderness area.

15

Taylor Creek
Visitors Center

The Park

The Taylor Creek Visitor Center was constructed in 1968 to serve the United States Forest Service campgrounds and parks in the Lake Tahoe Basin. The Visitors Center is open every day from Memorial Day to Labor Day and weekends in October and hosts some 400,000 visitors annually.

The Walks

Four short nature trails are available to canine hikers at the Visitors Center. The newly renovated Rainbow Trail covers a half-mile and emphasizes the importance of marshes and meadows to the clarity of Lake Tahoe. This is a paved asphalt trail. The Lake of the Sky Trail leads to the south shore of Lake Tahoe; it is 3/8 mile long. Smokey's Trail is just a few steps at 1/8 mile and is devoted to safe campfire construction. The marquee trail at Taylor's Creek is the Stream Profile Chamber Trail. It is a delightful jaunt through a Jeffrey pine forest into a mountain meadow bursting with wildflowers in the spring and early summer, and then across a marsh. A large viewing platform overlooks the marsh and

Lake Tahoe - East Shore

Distance from downtown Reno
- 62 miles
Phone Number
- (530) 573-2674
Website
- www.r5.fs.fed.us/ltbmu/visitor/ taylor_creek/
Admission Fee
- None
Directions
- Take Virginia Street to Interstate 80 and head east to Highway 395. Go south towards Carson City. Follow Highway 395 through the Mount Rose Interchange taking heed of the signs to Carson City. Continue through the capital and on to US 50, in the south end of Carson City. Turn right on US 50, and continue through South Lake Tahoe to the "Y," where Highway 50 merges with Highway 89. Turn right on Highway 89, and follow north about 3.5 miles to the entrance on your right. The entrance and parking areas are on the lake side of the highway.

meadow. The Stream Profile Chamber is a diverted section of Taylor's Creek viewed through aquarium-like windows (your dog will have to wait while you duck in for the show). Interpretive markers provide information on the plant and animal life along the path.

Dog Friendliness

Dogs are welcome to explore the nature trails of Taylor's Creek Visitor Center.

Traffic

Summer crowds are intense and even worse when the salmon run in the fall. No bikes are allowed on these trails.

Canine Swimming

No swimming on these canine hikes but there are plenty of dog-dunking holes nearby.

Trail Time

Less than an hour.

16

Peavine Peak
Trails

The Park

Peavine Peak, the hefty mountain dominating northwest Reno, is named for the wild peavines found growing in areas of natural springs. Washo Indians came here to camp and you can still see rounded depressions in boulders that were used to grind food. In 1913 the American Land Conservancy brokered a deal to put much of Peavine Peak into public use in perpetuity, wresting many tracts from its top section from private hands.

Reno

Distance from downtown Reno
  - 2 miles
Phone Number
  - (775) 298-0012
Website
  - www.jour.unr.edu/outpost/
  outdoors/archives/
  out.trent.peav2.html
Admission Fee
  - None
Directions
  - Take Virginia Street north to McCarran Boulevard. Turn left on McCarran and follow to Kings Row, turn right. Follow Kings Row to the top of the hill to the park, and park in the parking lot. The trailhead is back along Kings Row where it dead-ends at dirt. Look for and follow the Forest Service Road 658 signs.

The Walks

Peavine is riddled with access roads, jeep tracks and trails. The climb to the summit - with its television towers - features an elevation gain of about 3,000 feet to the 8,266-foot peak. Heading up Keystone Canyon the route is steep and less energetic dogs may favor the Kings Row trailhead at Hilltop Park. The complete distance to the top is 10 miles. Look for mule deer that use the area as a stopover on their migration from California. Peavine Peak features desert sage-covered slopes, aspen groves, pine forests and rolling meadows.

Dog Friendliness

Dogs can hike the trails on Peavine Peak.

Traffic

Mountain bikers love these trails and fast-moving bikes are a definite trail hazard, especially on the lower flanks.

Canine Swimming

There are some creeks and ponds on Peavine, but most tend to be on private property.

Trail Time

More than an hour.

17

Bartley Ranch Park

The Park

Bartley Ranch was a working ranch in Southwest Reno for many years, where the owners raised horses and cattle. Some of the historic farm equipment can still be seen in the 56-acre county park, built in the mid-1990s. Already containing a full size horse arena and a 400-seat amphitheater used for outdoor concerts and performances, Bartley Ranch is continuing to expand and add features. As you enter the park, you'll drive across a covered bridge leading to the interpretive center and the hiking trails.

Reno

Distance from downtown Reno
- 4 miles
Phone Number
- (775) 828-6612
Website
- www.bartleyranch.com/
Admission Fee
- None
Directions
- From downtown Reno take Virginia Street south to California Avenue. Turn right on California and follow west to Plumas Street. Turn left on Plumas, follow to McCarran Boulevard and turn left. Follow one block to Lakeside, then turn right. Follow Lakeside about a half a mile to the park entrance, on the left.

The Walks

Bartley Ranch maintains more than two miles of hiking trails for you and your dog. The nature trail winding along a low ridge is not too steep and ideal for canine hikers of any ability. The sandy trails are especially paw-friendly. There are few shade trees, however, as yet in this new park so hiking expeditions will be fully exposed to the sun.

Dog Friendliness

Dogs are welcome in the park.

Traffic

The trails are comparatively uncrowded.

Canine Swimming

There is nowhere for your dog to swim at Bartley Ranch.

Trail Time

Less than an hour.

18

Squaw Valley

The Park

Trappers named this area "Squaw Valley" when they discovered only women and children, gathering food for the coming winter, living here. When Placer County Surveyor Thomas Young came to work in the valley in 1856, he was suitably impressed. He wrote, "Squaw Valley is the most beautiful valley the eye of man has ever beheld." Alexander Cushing, a Wall Street lawyer, first saw this paradise on crutches, after breaking his ankle on a ski trip to Sugar Bush in 1946. He came back in 1949 with $400,000 and opened a ski resort on Thanksgiving Day. The amenities were few: a choice of two rope tows, the world's largest double chairlift called Squaw One and an unfinished lodge. Today, more than a half-century later, Squaw Valley is a world famous, two-season resort.

Lake Tahoe - North Shore

Distance from downtown Reno
- 42 miles
Phone Number
- (530) 583-6985
Website
- www.summer.squaw.com/html/hiking.html
Admission Fee
- None
Directions
- Take Interstate 80 west toward Truckee, until you reach the Highway 89, Tahoe City exit. Turn left and go under the bridge, then continue on Highway 89 south to Squaw Valley, about 6 miles.

The Walks

The summer hiking trails all begin at High Camp at the top of the Cable Car ride. One of the easiest is High Camp Loop, which is about a mile long, and only gains about 150 feet in elevation. The hike to the top of the Links chair lift and back to High Camp traipses through a mountain meadow filled with wildflowers. For more strenuous hikes, take the dog to the Top Terminal of Emigrant Chair, a 1.5-mile climb to

360-degree views, or the 460-foot elevation gain to Newport Chair and views of the Palisades, a favorite cliff of extreme skiers. In the other direction, steep trails lead down Shirley Canyon to Shirley Lake. You can also hike down into the valley from High Camp; it is a 2000-foot elevation loss from High Camp via the ski path.

Dog Friendliness

Dogs are allowed on the Cable Car, and are welcome at the Full Moon and Stargazer hikes. Because of the crowds on July 4th, dogs are not allowed that day.

Traffic

Bikes are allowed on these trails, which aren't as crowded with hikers as they are with skiers.

Canine Swimming

There is canine swimming on the High Camp trails at Squaw Valley.

Trail Time

More than an hour.

19

Loch Leven Lakes

The Park

The builders of the Central Pacific Railroad struggled through this area in 1868-69 to lay tracks for the first Transcontinental Railroad - hikers cross the tracks as they climb to Lower Loch Leven Lake. The laborers, mostly imported Chinese, worked tirelessly, even through the winter under great snow sheds, to link east to west in America. Today, the tracks follow the same route as the original Central Pacific did, and are used by the Union Pacific Railroad.

Lake Tahoe - North Shore

Distance from downtown Reno
  - 55 miles
Phone Number
  - (530) 265-4531
Website
  - www.r5.fs.fed.us/tahoe/pdf/ LochLevenROG.pdf
Admission Fee
  - None
Directions
  - Take Virginia Street to Interstate 80, and head west through Truckee to the Big Bend exit. Follow Big Bend Road to the Visitors Center and park there for the trailhead.

The Walks

Look around the trailhead when you start this hike at about 5,700 feet in elevation. Once part of the Overland Emigrant Trail used by settlers forging West, faint rust marks from iron wagon wheels can still be seen here and there. For a short hike, the trail to the lower lake is about 2.6 miles. If you go on to the upper lakes it is another mile. This moderately difficult trail begins by following the frontage road, then snakes through a steady climb among rough granite outcroppings. Soon you enter a meadow rich in vegetation and wildflowers and eventually across the Union Pacific tracks and up to a ridge where you discover the lakes. From Lower Leven Lake the lake trail continues on to the middle and upper lakes and a side spur leads to Salmon Lake.

Dog Friendliness

Dogs are permitted on the trails across this United States Forest Service land.

Traffic

There is the reward of solitude waiting on these trails, especially after summer ends.

Canine Swimming

Dogs will enjoy refreshing dog paddling about in any of the Loch Leven area lakes.

Trail Time

More than an hour.

How To Pet A Dog
Tickling tummies slowly and gently works
wonders. Never use a rubbing motion; this
makes dogs bad-tempered. A gentle tickle with
the tips of the fingers is all that is necessary to
induce calm in a dog. I hate strangers who go
up to dogs with their hands held to the dog's
nose, usually palm towards themselves. How
does the dog know that the hand doesn't hold
something horrid? The palm should always be
shown to the dog and go straight down to
between the dog's front legs and tickle gently
with a soothing voice to acompany the action.
Very often the dog raises its back leg in a
scratching movement, it gets so much pleasure
from this.
-Barbara Woodhouse

20

Verdi Nature Study Area

The Park

Verdi was created as a stop on the Central Pacific Railroad as the line made its way into Nevada. After the railroad arrived, Verdi evolved into a major shipping center for lumber and railroad ties gleaned from the forested peaks surrounding the town. A large fire devastated Verdi in 1926 and the town never recovered. A few of the original buildings still stand in the downtown area. The Verdi Nature Study Area was built in the late 1990s as an outdoor classroom for local schools.

Verdi

Distance from downtown Reno
- 11 miles
Phone Number
- (775) 334-3808
Website
www.nevadadivisionofwildlife.org/con_ed/verdi.htm
Admission Fee
- None
Directions
- From downtown Reno take Virginia Street to Interstate 80. Head west to the Verdi exit (Exit 5). Follow the road to Bridge Street, about 3 miles, and turn right. Follow to the Verdi Elementary School; the Nature Trail begins in the back of the school.

The Walks

Verdi Nature Trail is a half-mile loop trail on paw-friendly packed sand. In this unique environment where the Great Basin meets the Sierra Nevada, the different desert habitats readily distinguish themselves from the lusher mountain zones. You pass through sagebrush flats edged with large black pines. Along the trail are colorful wildflowers and native plants, and the remains of an old logging flume. The trail is very easy to walk and makes a great outing for your dog.

Dog Friendliness

Dogs are welcome in the Verdi Nature Study Area; their scent helps keep mountain lions away from the park.

Traffic

This charming park is often empty and you and the dog will likely be sharing the rushing waters of the Truckee River with only songbirds.

Canine Swimming

Dogs can wade and splash in the Truckee River.

Trail Time

Less than an hour.

21
Idlewild Park

The Park

Idlewild Park is one of the oldest parks in Reno. The California Building, on the south side of the park, was built in 1927 to help celebrate the highway exposition. Its California Mission architecture is a harbinger of West Coast style in the early part of the 20th century. In 1939, the California Building became the home of the Reno Art Center. In the 1930s Idlewild Park included a small zoo with buffalo, bears and monkeys. Today the most exotic creatures you are likely to see in the 49-acre park are ducks, geese and skateboarders.

The Walks

The main trail through Idlewild Park is the paved bike path that is part of the Truckee River Walk. There are some pathways and many stopping places leading off the main drag as it meanders along the water, but this is where most people walk their dogs in the park. There is also fragrant dogwalking to be had in the Rose Garden near the historic California Building.

Dog Friendliness

Idlewild Park is a splendid meet-and-greet spot for dogs.

Traffic

Canine hikers will be sharing the park with picknickers, ballplayers and all types of wheeled conveyances on the paved path.

Canine Swimming

The trail hugs the Truckee River with plenty of places for the dog to test her paddling stroke. Watch out for swift currents.

Trail Time

Less than an hour.

*"If you pick up a starving dog and make him prosperous,
he will not bite you; that is the principal
difference between a dog and a man."*
- Mark Twain

22

Cascade Creek Falls

The Park

Cascade Lake, as were all the lakes in the Tahoe area, was scraped out thousands of years ago by retreating glaciers. The thundering Cascade Creek Falls, with a 200-foot plunge, add an exclamation mark to the area's popularity.

The Walks

The hike to Cascade Creek Falls is a one-mile out-and-back linear trail with a modest 150-foot elevation gain. The wide and often dusty trail winds through a shady white fir and Jeffrey pine forest that hosts scenic views of Cascade Lake, Emerald Bay and Lake Tahoe. The last part of the trail is very rocky and the final 100 yards clambors over glacially polished granite slabs. Watch your dog's footing here. Seclusion from this very popular trail awaits further up the canyon on the way to Snow and Azure lakes.

Lake Tahoe/West Shore

Distance from downtown Reno
- 65 miles
Phone Number
- (530) 573-2600
Website
- www.r5.fs.fed.us/ltbmu/visitor/hiking/west.htm
Admission Fee
- None
Directions
- Take Virginia Street to Interstate 80 East to Highway 395 and south to Carson City. Stay on Highway 395 through the Mount Rose Interchange; following the signs to Carson City. Continue through Carson City to US 50 on the south end of the city. Turn right on US 50, and continue through South Lake Tahoe to the "Y," where US 50 merges with Highway 89. Turn right on Highway 89 and follow north about 8 miles to the Bayview Campground across from Inspiration Point. Parking is located at the far end of the campground.

Dog Friendliness

Dogs are welcome on the trails in the Cascade Lake area.

Traffic

This is a good trail if you enjoy communal hiking, especially in high summer.

Canine Swimming

Cascade Creek is not the place for your dog to show off his aquatic talents.

Trail Time

Less than an hour.

23
Tahoe Rim Trail

The Park

The idea of a footpath completely around America's largest alpine lake first came to Glenn Hampton shortly after he arrived in Lake Tahoe in 1977. Hampton, an officer with the United States Forest Service, drew up plans for just such a trail as part of a graduate program he took in outdoor recreation in 1980. The federal government did not have the financial resources to implement a large-scale program of this type but gave Hampton the go-ahead to start pursuing his "impossible dream." He began building a coalition of fellow believers in the 150-mile trail and eventually more than 10,000 volunteers would work 200,000 hours and donate thousands of dollars before the trail was completely finished in 2001. The Tahoe Rim Trail visits two states, six counties, three national forests, state parkland and three wilderness areas and is one of the largest volunteer projects ever completed in the United States. An estimated 3,000 people each week use the trail, marked by triangular blue markers, during the summer and fall. The Tahoe Rim Trail opens when the snow melts in late spring and closes with the October snows.

Lake Tahoe/East Shore

Distance from downtown Reno
- 50 miles
Phone Number
- (775) 298-0012
Website
- www.tahoerimtrail.org/newtrt.htm
Admission Fee
- None
Directions
- Take Virginia Street to Interstate 80 East to Highway 395 south towards Carson City. Go through the Mount Rose Interchange, following the signs to Carson City. Continue through Carson City to the US 50 Lake Tahoe turnoff, which is past Carson City on the right. Turn right, and follow US 50 up the mountain to Spooner Lake, about 9 miles. You'll see a dirt pull off next to the Spooner Lake sign on the right, pull off and park there, the trailhead begins at this dirt parking area.

The Walks

There are eight trailheads with parking around Lake Tahoe with access to the Tahoe Rim Trail. The lowest point of the ridge-running route is 6300 feet at Tahoe City and the trail reaches its apex at Relay Peak, topping out at 10,333 feet. One of the trail's most popular legs is between Spooner Lake and the Tahoe Meadows - a 21-mile hike with no more than a 10% grade in any spot. Most of this canine hike, that passes through dense forests and open meadows, is on soft, sandy terrain.

Dog Friendliness

Dogs are welcome on the Tahoe Rim Trail.

Traffic

Foot traffic and equestrians are permitted on all 150 miles of the trail; mountain bikes are restricted in some areas, mostly in the southwest and northeast legs around the lake.

Canine Swimming

You are never too far from a refreshing doggie dip on the Tahoe Rim Trail.

Trail Time

More than an hour - maybe more than a week for a complete circumnavigation of Lake Tahoe.

24

Meeks Bay

The Park

Meeks Bay has been a resort on the west shore of Lake Tahoe for over 100 years, but before that, it had a varied ranching history. In 1862, the Meeks brothers cut 25 tons of wild hay from the surrounding meadows, and in 1878 the two men ran a dairy herd. They summered the cows in Meeks Bay, and wintered them in Coloma, near Sacramento. The bay was an important summer gathering place for the Washo Indians, and in 1997, 300 acres around Meeks Bay was leased back to the Washo Tribe. Today, the tribe operates the Meeks Bay Resort and Marina.

Lake Tahoe - West Shore

Distance from downtown Reno
- 78 miles
Phone Number
- (530) 573-2600
Website
- www.r5.fs.fed.us/ltbmu/visitor/ hiking/west.htm
Admission Fee
- None
Directions
- From downtown Reno take Interstate 80 East to Highway 395 and south towards Carson City. Use Highway 395 through the Mount Rose Interchange, following the signs to Carson City. Continue through Carson City, to US 50 on the south end of town. Turn right on US 50, and continue through South Lake Tahoe to the "Y," where US 50 merges with Highway 89. Turn right on Highway 89 and follow north to the Meeks Bay Resort. Parking is located across the highway from the resort at a small dirt parking lot.

The Walks

This is a moderate trail with steady climbing much of the way. The route follows a wide, flat dirt road for the first mile or so, until it reaches a sign marking entry into the Desolation Wilderness, where the real canine hiking begins. The trail parallels Meeks Creek and is draped with mixed conifers - Douglas fir, red fir, pines, cedar and, some believe, Sequoias, which are found nowhere else around the lake. The total ascent to Phipp's pass is 1400 feet and 4.5 miles one way.

Dog Friendliness

Dogs are allowed on this arboreal hike.

Traffic

This hike is demanding enough to make traffic on the trail sparse.

Canine Swimming

Although Meeks Creek is often scarcely deep enough for trout there is good splashing to be had here.

Trail Time

More than an hour.

"We are alone, absolutely alone on this chance planet; and, amid all the forms of life that surround us, not one, excepting the dog, has made an alliance with us."
- Maurice Maeterlinck

25

Washoe Lake State Park

The Park

Washoe Lake was the ancestral winter home for the Washo Indians, where they came after a summer at Lake Tahoe. When mines brought white settlement to the area two ore mills operated here - the ruins of the New York Mill are still visible near Little Washoe Lake. The State of Nevada moved to protect the Washoe Valley in 1977 with the creation of this park, preserving 8,053 acres on the western edge of the Virginia Range.

The Walks

Trails abound in Washoe Lake State Park, from narrow walks in the sagebrush on the hillside across from the main park to sandy hikes where your dog can romp along the edge of the lake. An easy one-mile hike to Deadman's Creek leaves from the large dead tree on Eastlake Boulevard, a few hundred feet from the park entrance. In the wetlands, which are off-limits from February 1 to July 15 for bird nesting, a one-mile interpretive loop explains plant and animal highlights in the park.

Carson City

Distance from downtown Reno
- 18 miles
Phone Number
- (775) 687-4319
Website
- www.state.nv.us/stparks/wl.htm
Admission Fee
- None
Directions
- Take Virginia Street to Interstate 80 and go west to Highway 395. Take Highway 395 south towards Carson City. At the Mount Rose Interchange, follow the signs for Carson City, south. Stay on Highway 395 south to the Eastlake Boulevard turn on the left. Turn left on Eastlake, and follow to the park. Soon after you turn on Eastlake, you'll see Little Washoe Lake on your right. The main park area is two miles further on Eastlake.

Dog Friendliness

Dogs are allowed on the trails and beaches.

Traffic

The trails are much less crowded than the recreational places in the park.

Canine Swimming

The lakes and creeks at Washoe Lake State Park are all good swimming holes for your dog.

Trail Time

More than an hour.

26
Echo Lakes

The Park

Echo Lake, off Echo Summit (7,400 feet), is a pristine alpine lake on the crest of the Sierra Nevada. This trail is yet another gateway into the Desolation Wilderness. Echo Summit was an important part of the "Bonanza Trail" between Virginia City, Nevada and Placerville, California. Once this area of the trail was completed, wagons had a much easier trip between the two towns, and commerce grew quickly. Echo Summit is the highest point on US 50 between Placerville and Lake Tahoe.

The Walks

The out-and-back hike to the north side of Echo Lake covers 2.5 miles and is a good flat walk, without many paw-piercing rocks. This trip can be eliminated entirely by hitching a ride on the water taxi. From the taxi landing, the next 3/4 mile goes up 400 feet. A full trip out to Aloha Lake is 3.5 miles from the landing and visits many other lakes in the region, including Ralston, Tamarack and Lake of the Woods.

Echo Lakes - South Shore

Distance from downtown Reno
- 71 miles
Phone Number
- (530) 573-2600
Website
- www.r5.fs.fed.us/ltbmu/visitor/hiking/south.htm
Admission Fee
- None
Directions
- Take Virginia Street to Interstate 80 and drive east to Highway 395. Go south towards Carson City. Follow Highway 395 through the Mount Rose Interchange by tracking the signs to Carson City. Continue through Carson City, to US 50, on the south end of the capital. Turn right on US 50, and continue through South Lake Tahoe to the "Y," where US 50 merges with Highway 89. Turn left on US 50 and follow past Meyers to Echo Summit and turn onto Johnson Pass Road. Stay left and the road will lead to the parking area by Lower Echo Lake.

Dog Friendliness
Dogs are welcome on the trail to Aloha Lake.

Traffic
As you continue deeper into the wilderness, the trails become more rocky and less crowded.

Canine Swimming
Dogs can look forward to a frisky swim here - remember the water is only warm on top.

Trail Time
More than an hour.

27

Long Lake

The Park

This region of the Sierra is far different from the area surrounding Lake Tahoe. More granite boulders and glaciated landscape dominate the landscape of the High Sierra. Many of the lakes in the area look like bowls scooped out of the granite. One such lake is Long Lake. This land is managed by the United States Forest Service in the Tahoe National Forest - a total of 811,740 acres. It is estimated there are more mining claims within Tahoe Forest boundaries than any other national forest.

The Walks

The easy ramble to Long Lake starts from the parking lot, where you will clambor down a steep slope and cross the dam to the beginning of the trail. About 1/2 mile up the footpath, a sign points the way to the Palisade Creek Trail and its ultimate destination of Heath Falls. This is a 5-mile out-and-back trail and is steep going. The trail crosses several granite areas that could be hard on your dog. Passing up the journey to Heath Falls, the main stem trail leads straight to

Truckee

Distance from downtown Reno
 - 53 miles
Phone Number
 - (530) 587-3887
Website
 - None
Admission Fee
 - None
Directions
 - Take Interstate 80 west toward Truckee and past Donner Summit to the Soda Springs/ Norden exit. Turn left onto Old Highway 40, cross the freeway, follow 1 mile to the signal and turn right onto Soda Springs Road. Cross the railroad tracks, and follow to Pahatsi, another mile. Turn right on Pahatsi. After less than a mile, by the entrance to Royal Gorge Cross-Country Ski Area, the pavement ends, and the road changes to Kidd Lake Road. Follow Kidd Lake Road another 3.8 miles past Camp Pahatsi then across the dam below Kidd Lake. Shortly after passing the Royal Gorge Devil's Lookout warming hut on your right, take the left fork and continue 1/2 mile farther to the parking area/trailhead.

Long Lake. At the far end of the lake are views of Royal Gorge Canyon and the headwaters of the North Fork of the American River.

Dog Friendliness

Dogs are permitted on the trails in the Tahoe National Forest.

Traffic

These trails, especially the ten-mile round trip to Heath Falls, will leave crowds far behind.

Canine Swimming

Long Lake is a superb doggie swimming hole.

Trail Time

More than an hour.

"My dog can bark like a Congressman, fetch like an aide, beg like a press secretary and play dead like a receptionist."
- Gerald Solomon

28

Dayton State Park

The Park

Dayton is one of Nevada's first permanent settlements; a trading post was built by Spafford Hall of Indiana on the banks of Gold Creek in 1852. When 200 Chinese workers were brought here to dig a water ditch, the town became known as Chinatown. In 1861 the name changed to Dayton after John Day, who surveyed the area. That same year the Rock Point Mill was built to process ore from the Comstock Lode mines. Traces of the mill are still visible in the western side of the 160-acre Dayton State Park.

Dayton

Distance from downtown Reno
- 44 miles
Phone Number
- (775) 687-5678
Website
- www.state.nv.us/stparks/dsp.htm
Admission Fee
- None
Directions
- Take Virginia Street to Interstate 80 West to Highway 395. Follow Highway 395 south and head to Carson City, following the Carson City signs at the Mount Rose Interchange. Follow through town to US 50. Turn left on US 50 and follow through the town of Dayton to the park. The park will be on your left, and the camping and picnicking facilities on your right.

The Walks

There are several trails through the park, including the Mill Site Trail. The best canine hike here is the Carson River Trail; flat and sandy, with a grand view of the water and the town of Dayton. Mature cottonwoods thriving in the moist soil along the Carson River shade much of the quiet walk.

Dog Friendliness

Dogs are welcome to explore Dayton State Park.

Traffic

This small park can get busy on summer weekends.

Canine Swimming

It will be hard to keep a water-loving dog out of the peacefully flowing Carson River.

Trail Time

Less than an hour.

"Ever consider what they must think of us?
I mean, here we come back from the grocery store
with the most amazing haul - chicken, pork,
half a cow...They must think we're the
greatest hunters on earth!"

- Anne Tyler

29

Boca Reservoir

The Park

Prosser, Stampede, and Boca Lakes are man-made and comprise the Truckee Storage Project, which helps provide water to Reno and Sparks. Boca sprouted as a railroad town at the mouth of the Little Truckee and Truckee River ("Boca" means "mouth" in Spanish). Residents also commercially harvested ice from the rivers in winter for the Trout Creek Ice Company beginning in 1897. The ice was packed in sawdust or hay and shipped by rail as far away as New Orleans. The town was active from 1867 through 1927, but today only the remnants you see on the trail remain of the town. Boca Dam was built in 1937 as part of the Truckee River Agreement to manage water between Nevada and California.

Truckee

Distance from downtown Reno
- 26 miles
Phone Number
- (530) 587-3558
Website
- www.r5.fs.fed.us/tahoe/tkrd/ tnftruckeerec.html#day%20use
Admission Fee
- None
Directions
- Take Interstate 80 west past the Hirschdale Exit to the Boca/ Stampede exit. Turn left off the freeway, and follow Boca Road to the Town Site trail, which will be on your right. Boca Reservoir is about a mile beyond the trail, and Stampede Reservoir is seven miles farther on.

The Walks

The Boca Townsite Trail is the perfect place to begin your exploration of this area with your dog. The one-mile paved asphalt trail leaves from the

gravel parking lot and climbs gently up the side of a hill to the townsite and a small cemetery. Interpretive kiosks with historical photographs show the town of Boca as it appeared when still vibrant. After you soak up the area's history you can sample the numerous trails and dirt roads throughout the Boca, Prosser and Stampede vicinity.

Dog Friendliness

Dogs are welcome on these United States Forest Service trails.

Traffic

These trails are lightly used unless it is a weekend.

Canine Swimming

There is no swimming along the Townsite Trail, but there are numerous access points to the reservoirs for canine aquatics.

Trail Time

The Boca Townsite Trail requires less than an hour although you can find plenty of additional hikes in the area.

"Children are for people who can't have dogs."
-Anonymous

30

Truckee River Bike Path

The Park

As long ago as the 1860s Tahoe was a favorite place for wealthy San Franciscans to spend their summers, and mansions began to spring up along the lake shore. Tahoe City was founded as a lumber center on the lake, but soon blossomed into a bristling tourist center when the Tahoe House Hotel was built in 1863. The Truckee River Bike Path follows the Truckee River from Tahoe City, where it begins flowing out of Lake Tahoe, to Squaw Valley. Lake Tahoe is fed by 63 tributaries but the Truckee River is its only outlet.

Tahoe City

Distance from downtown Reno
- 47.5 miles
Phone Number
- None
Website
- www.greatbasinbicycles.com/
Maps/truckee_river_bike_
path.htm
Admission Fee
- No
Directions
- Take Interstate 80 West towards Truckee, to Highway 89, Tahoe City exit. Turn left and go under the bridge, then continue on Highway 89 south, past Squaw Valley to Tahoe City, and the junction of Highway 28. You'll find plenty of parking in Tahoe City on Highway 89, or just around the corner on Highway 28 about a quarter of a mile, where there is a paved parking lot and the bike path starts.

The Walks

The Truckee River Bike Path is a flat, paved asphalt path and easy trotting for any dog. The route travels through marshlands, meadows and alpine forests. During the summer you can watch brightly hued rafts and kayaks navigating the rushing waters and calm pools of the Truckee River. If you do the entire round trip between Tahoe City and Squaw Valley you will have a healthy canine hike of 10 miles.

Dog Friendliness

Dogs are permitted to trot on this popular multi-use trail.

Traffic

The scenery is so spectacular along the Truckee River Bike Path, the trail can at times seem like a department store checkout line with all the crowds. Lighter traffic can be found in the shoulder seasons of spring and fall.

Canine Swimming

A canine hike with a water-loving dog on the Truckee Rivr Bike Path will be a definite stop-and-go trip with plenty of access to the river.

Trail Time

More than an hour.

31
Mt. Judah Loop

The Park

People have been trying to plot passageways across the rugged, snow-choked Sierra Nevadas for thousands of years. The Nisenan and Washo tribes plied these lands for food, water and recreation long before American emigrants in wagon trains set out from St. Louis headed for a mountain pass. The Tahoe National Forest, straddling the crest of the Sierra Nevada on more than one million acres, is managed today by the U.S. Forest Service. There are more than 400 miles of hiking trails in the national forest.

Truckee

Distance from downtown Reno
- 60 miles
Phone Number
- (530) 587-3558
Website
- www.r5.fs.fed.us/tahoe/pdf/pctmtjudah.pdf
Admission Fee
- None
Directions
- Take Virginia Street to Interstate 80 and go west through Truckee to the Castle Peak Area/Boreal Ridge Road exit. On the south side of the highway you'll see a Tahoe National Forest Trailhead sign. Park at the trailhead and follow the directions on the sign, turning east for .4 mile to the trailhead. Don't park at the Visitors Center on Interstate 80, you can't leave your car there unattended.

The Walks

The Mt. Judah Loop is a 4.5-mile round trip detour off the Pacific Crest Trail and is the main trail to Donner Peak. This is a difficult trail, especially beyond Donner Pass, with a rocky rise over 1200 feet to a peak elevation of 8,245 feet. The dog will be trotting among massive granite boulders smoothed by the movement of glacial ice. There are rewarding views on the way up and outstanding looks of prominent peaks - Anderson, Castle Peaks, the red face of Red Mountain - waiting at the top of the ridge. In mid-summer the east face of Mt. Judah is covered with the exquisite purple color of Rock Fringe flowers.

Dog Friendliness

Dogs are welcome to climb through these historic mountain passes.

Traffic

The Mt. Judah loop gets heavy use summer and winter - it is a popular snowshoeing and cross-country ski area.

Canine Swimming

There is no canine swimming along the Mt. Judah loop.

Trail Time

More than an hour.

"Dog. A kind of additional or subsidiary Diety designed to catch the overflow and surplus of the world's worship."
- Ambrose Bierce

32

Carson Pass

The Park

Carson Pass, at 8,754 feet, is one of the most beautiful high-mountain passes in the Sierra. The pass gets its name from hunter and trapper Christopher "Kit" Carson. John Fremont hired Carson as a guide and his company made the first successful winter crossing of the Sierra in 1844. It is likely that Fremont's men went not through the exact notch of Carson Pass but used a point a mile or so south. Regardless, the pass was not named by Fremont or Carson; in 1844 it was called simply "The Pass." Adventurers seeking gold in 1849 named the passageway "Carson Pass."

Lake Tahoe - South Shore

Distance from downtown Reno
- 78 miles
Phone Number
- (530) 573-2674
Website
- www.r5.fs.fed.us/ltbmu/visitor wilderness/mokelumne.htm
Admission Fee
- Permit required for wilderness hiking
Directions
- Take Virginia Street to Interstate 80. Go east to Highway 395 and head south towards Carson City. Follow Highway 395 through the Mount Rose Interchange, using the signs to Carson City as your guide. Continue through Carson City and beyond until you reach Highway 88 (Carson Pass). Turn right and follow to the parking area on the right, at the crest of Carson Pass.

The Walks

The trail from Carson Pass leads to a string of jeweled alpine lakes, the most popular being emerald green Winnemucca Lake. This is a wide, sandy trail with no steep climbs for a little more than a mile. The alpine forest gives way to mountain meadows with a profusion of summer lupine, mules ear and Indian paintbrush. Another mile further and 400 feet higher is Round Top Lake; Round Top Mountain in the background can also be scaled. Going out 4.5 miles on the leads to 4th of July Lake, a depression filled with clear Sierra snow melt. This path loses 1000 feet of elevation in a hurry to views of Summit City Canyon.

Dog Friendliness

Dogs are permitted on this Forest Service trail.

Traffic

The easy path to Winnemucca Lake is well trod; with a few hundred more yards of canine hiking you can lose the crowds.

Canine Swimming

Swimming in these cold water mountain lakes is a frosty treat for hiking dogs.

Trail Time

More than an hour.

*"My dog is worried about the economy
because Alpo is up to 99 cents a can.
That's almost $7.00 in dog money."*
- *Joe Weinstein*

97

33

Stateline Lookout

The Park

Although this lookout is no longer staffed, many other lookouts in the Lake Tahoe Basin remain in use during the summer with rangers scouring the treetops for signs of fire. The Stateline Lookout has become a popular and much-used trail in the North Lake Tahoe area.

The Walks

A short half-mile hike leads to the lookout along a paved asphalt trail. Interpretive signs discuss the history of the area and the native plants growing near the path.

Dog Friendliness

Dogs are welcome to come along on this walk and have a look around.

Lake Tahoe - North Shore

Distance from downtown Reno
- 36 miles
Phone Number
- (530) 573-2600
Website
- www.r5.fs.fed.us/ltbmu/visitor/ hiking/north & east.htm
Admission Fee
- None
Directions
- Take Virginia Street to Interstate 80 and go east to Highway 395 and south towards Carson City. Follow Highway 395 to the Mount Rose Interchange and bear right to Highway 431, the Mount Rose Highway. Follow Highway 431 to where it ends at Highway 28, and turn right, towards North Lake Tahoe. Follow Highway 28 to Reservoir Drive, just east of the old Tahoe Biltmore Casino, turn right on Reservoir Drive, and follow north to Lakeview Avenue. Turn right on Lakeview Avenue and left on Forest Service Road 1601 (by the iron pipe gate). Park in the parking lot just below the lookout.

Traffic

This is a popular trail with summer strollers. Try it in the fall when the aspens change their color to a more select audience.

Canine Swimming

No swimming for the dog here.

Trail Time

Less than an hour.

34

Eagle Falls and Eagle Lake

The Park

Emerald Bay, with its dark green waters, is a must-see for visitors to Lake Tahoe. Originally called Eagle Bay, due to the nesting of eagles high above the lake, this is a turnaround point for lake steamers. Eagle Falls is the only waterfall that empties directly into Lake Tahoe.

The Walks

The climb to Eagle Falls is a hardy, one-mile ramble climaxing at Eagle Lake. A sandy trail leads to a rough and rocky staircase. A large footbridge crosses over Eagle Creek, then climbs again to a respite of shade under a stand of white fir, about half way up. The trail continues ascending on the flat, sandy trail. Leave the crowds behind at the Falls - thunderous in spring - and head off to Middle Velma Lake, about 4 1/2 miles further on, but it is strenuous, and at times rocky, so be prepared if you choose to continue exploring.

Lake Tahoe - West Shore
Distance from downtown Reno - 70 miles Phone Number - (530) 573-1600 Website - www.r5.fs.fed.us/ltbmu/visitor/poi/emerald.htm Admission Fee - Parking fee Directions - Take Virginia Street to Interstate 80 and go east to Highway 395 and south toward Carson City. Follow Highway 395 through the Mount Rose Interchange heeding the signs to Carson City. Continue through Carson City, to US 50 on the south end of Carson City. Turn right on US 50, and continue through South Lake Tahoe to the "Y," where US 50 merges with Highway 89. Turn right on Highway 89, and follow to Emerald Bay, about 10 miles and find the parking lot for Eagle Falls, about .1 mile further on the left. If the lot is full, park in the view point parking lot. The trail to Eagle Lake leaves from the parking lot.

Dog Friendliness

Dogs can hike the trail to Eagle Falls and beyond.

Traffic

This can be a communal dog walk of near-ridiculous proportions; in summer tourist season you can hardly see the lake for the people.

Canine Swimming

Your dog can duck away from the crowds in Eagle Creek if it is not too cold.

Trail Time

More than an hour.

35

Frog Lake Overlook

The Park

The lakes and streams of the Castle Peak area are a favorite for hikers because they are easily accessed from Interstate 80 as it follows the Truckee River Canyon. This access inlcudes the Pacific Crest Trail featuring some of the best High Sierra scenery that can be reached quickly by local hikers. The land is part of the Truckee Ranger District of the Tahoe National Forest.

Truckee

Distance from downtown Reno
- 42 miles
Phone Number
- (530) 587-3558
Website
- None
Admission Fee
- None
Directions
- Take Interstate 80 west toward Truckee. Exit at Boreal Ridge, past the Castle Peak rest area. Follow the road back under the Interstate until it ends at the trailhead.

The Walks

The trail to Frog Lake Overlook is 6 miles roundtrip, and it is strenuous. At about 1/4 mile, the trail forks in three different directions, take the middle fork for Summit Lake. This part of the trail is flat, and if you don't want to hike all the way to the overlook, stay to the right here, and take the dog to Summit Lake, where you can enjoy the peaceful scenery. The left fork continues uphill under the forest canopy for about a mile, then bursts into a meadow that is ablaze in early summer with wildflowers. Another stout climb awaits across the meadow before the trail straightens out, and you can follow it to the overlook, and see a beautiful view of Frog Lake. Don't hike down, it's on private land.

Dog Friendliness

Dogs are welcome to test the trails on the way to Frog Lake.

Traffic

There is scant competition for the trails deep in the meadows on this canine hike.

Canine Swimming

If the water's up in Summit Lake, you dog can jump right in.

Trail Time

More than an hour.

"He is very imprudent, a dog is. He never makes it
his business to inquire whether you are in the
right or in the wrong, never bothers
as to whether you are going up or down
upon's life ladder, never asks whether you are
rich or poor, silly or wise, sinner or saint."
                                        - Jerome K. Jerome

36
Fort Churchill State Park

The Park

Alarmist reports of a so-called Pyramid Lake War between settlers and Indians led to the construction of Fort Churchill in 1861. It was designed to be a permanent installation with adobe buildings anchored to stone foundations, aligned in a square facing onto a central parade ground. An average of 200 soldiers were posted at the frontier fort, named for Sylvester Churchill, Inspector General of the United States Army. During the Civil War, Fort Churchill became an important supply depot for the Nevada Military District and was a troop base for patrols securing overland migration routes. But by 1870 the post was obsolete. Soldiers' graves were moved to Carson City and buildings were auctioned to the public for $750. Fort Churchill had not even lasted a decade. The state of Nevada acquired the land in 1932 and in 1957 it became a part of the State Park system. The state has not restored the park and the buildings survive in a state of arrested decay.

Carson City

Distance from downtown Reno
- 57
Phone Number
- (775) 577-2345
Website
- www.state.nv.us/stparks/fc.htm
Admission Fee
- Yes
Directions
- Take Virginia Street to Interstate 80, and head east to Fernley. Take the first Fernley exit, and follow through town to Highway 95A. Turn right, and follow Highway 95A south through Silver Springs and on to the park, which will be on your right.

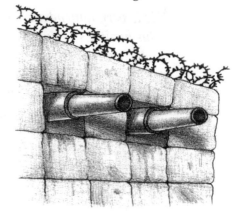

The Walks

Fort Churchill offers a variety of trails to enjoy with your dog. The best is the Carson River access trail, which scoots 16 miles between Fort Churchill and Lahontan State Recreation Area. This is an excellent walk, even in the summer, as much of the route is shaded with mature cottonwoods, and the river is always available for cooling off. There is also a network of other trails that connect with the Carson River trail, and the park system is continually developing new trails in the area. An interpretive trail with markers provides information about the fort ruins.

Dog Friendliness

Dogs are welcome to explore the park's 3200 aces and poke around the ruins of the old fort.

Traffic

These are quiet desert trails where you are more likely to find more wildlife than fellow travelers.

Canine Swimming

The Carson River, especially in the less rocky areas, is a first-rate canine swimming hole.

Trail Time

More than an hour.

37
Village Green

The Park

In the 1800s this area provided timber for support of the Comstock Lode in Virginia City. A 4,000-foot tramway ferried logs up and over the summit east of the village and a century later when an upscale town appeared here it became Incline Village. The town includes about 9,000 acres - including 2,400 acres of lake frontage - and 8,000 permanent residents. Village Green is the town's park, just one block from the beach.

Incline Village

Distance from downtown Reno
- 34 miles
Phone Number
- (775) 832-1100
Website
- None
Admission Fee
- None
Directions
- Take Virginia Street to Interstate 80, and head east to Highway 395. Follow Highway 395 south to the Mount Rose Interchange, and bear right off the freeway onto the Mount Rose Highway, State Highway 431. Follow Highway 431 west to Country Club Drive in Incline Village. Turn left on Country Club Drive, and follow to Lakeshore Drive. Then turn left.

The Walks

This grassy neighborhood park is perfect for a game of Frisbee and a romp with your dog. Dogs can be off leash as long as there are no organized or scheduled events happening on the Green. There are poop bags and poop scoops available. After Labor Day, the Incline Village beaches close, and residents take their dogs to Ski Beach for a romp in the lake off leash.

Dog Friendliness

Bring your dog down to the Green when coming to Incline Village.

Traffic

The Green can be a busy place in the summer.

Canine Swimming

You will need to leave the Green and walk the block to Lake Tahoe for a doggie dip in the off-season.

Trail Time

Less than an hour.

"If you don't think dogs can count, try putting three dog biscuits in your pocket and giving Fido two."

- Phil Pastoret

38

Dog Valley

The Park

The valley was a favored bypass for emigrants around Upper Truckee River Canyon. In some places in the valley you can still see the wheel ruts made by heavy Conestoga wagons heading West. The name "Dog Valley" came into popular use from the feral dogs that roamed the valley - abandoned by miners when the Comstock Lode played out and the boom-towns died.

The Walks

You can park your car where the pavement ends on

Verdi

Distance from downtown Reno
- 14 miles
Phone Number
- (530) 582-7892
Website
- None
Admission Fee
- None
Directions
- Take Virginia Street to Interstate 80 and go east to exit 5 in Verdi. Follow the road 3 miles and turn right on Bridge Street. Follow Bridge Street north to Dog Valley Road. Turn right again and follow the road to where the pavement ends, about 1 mile. You can park here, and walk up the trail, or take Dog Valley Road another 2.25 miles to the Forest Service Information Signs.

Dog Valley Road, and hike up the road, but the climb is steady and steep in places, and you'll be walking directly on the road, which is rough and rocky, and very dusty. Most people prefer to drive the 2.25 miles up to the plateau, and park at the Forest Service Information Signs. Then, you can choose from a variety of hikes that lead off from that central point. One popular canine hike follows the trail cut to maintain the power lines; it crosses the plateau then dips down into Dog Valley. Another short hike departs from the right of the information area, and walks out to the edge of the plateau, offering long views of Dog Valley and the Sierra beyond. This trail is soft and sandy, but soon drops down into Dog Valley, so the climb back up is steep. If you keep on Dog Valley Road, you'll reach Stampede Reservoir in about 10 miles.

Canine hikes in Dog Valley are a good opportunity to watch natural regeneration at work. In 1994, the Crystal Fire devastated the lower area of Dog Valley Road, and stark evidence of its passing still dominates the landscape. The area is slowly establishing itself again - Manzanita and native shrubs and grasses being the first to appear, they carpet the hillsides as you climb higher towards the plateau.

Dog Friendliness
Dogs are welcome in Dog Valley, hopefully in better circumstances than their outcast predecessors.

Traffic
This wilderness is close to Reno and a popular destination any time of year.

Canine Swimming
There is no swimming available on Dog Valley Road, unless you make it all the way to Stampede Rservoir.

Trail Time
More than an hour.

39
Northwest Urban Trails

The Park
While the development of Northwest Reno pushes rapidly towards Peavine Mountain, the city maintains open space behind the homes.

The Walks
There are plenty of good canine hikes in northwest Reno. Keystone Canyon is a sporty trail with access to the southern foothills on Peavine Mountain. Try the Northgate Loop that skirts the edge of Northgate Golf Course and

Reno

Distance from downtown Reno
- 5 miles
Phone Number
- (775) 334-2262
Website
- www.cityofreno.com/
com_service/parks/
park_planning/nwtrail/
Admission Fee
- None
Directions
- Take Virginia Street to Interstate 80, go west, exit at McCarran and turn right. Go to Mae Ann Drive and pick out your favorite trail on the Northwest Urban Trail map (on website).

can be extended for miles of exercise for the dog. Expect the footpaths to vary from flat and sandy to rough and rocky. There is not a lot of shade in summer; most of the paths wind through nothing but native sagebrush and rabbitbrush.

Dog Friendliness
These informal paths are built for your dog to run over.

Traffic
The rough trails of the Peavine foothills are extremely popular with mountain bikers but there are miles of trails here to spread out and escape to.

Canine Swimming
The trail hugs the Truckee River with plenty of places for the dog to test her paddling stroke. Watch out for swift currents.

Trail Time
Less than an hour.

"Properly trained, a man can be dog's best friend."
- Corey Ford

40
Virginia City Cemeteries

The Park

Virginia City was once the "Richest Place on Earth" and Nevada's most populous city with 20,000 silver-hungry residents looking to cash in on the great vein of ore that ran in the Comstock Lode. The entire town is a National Historic Site, the largest such federally maintained site in America. Now Virginia City looks much as it did at the height of the boom in the 1870s. While the buildings look the same, the cemeteries place the people who lived here in their roles as well. As Virginia City society was segregated - by religion, occupation, ethnicity - so too, were its cemeteries. This series of five distinct cemeteries are clumped together on a hill outside of town.

The Walks

There are plenty of jeep trails to explore with your dog

Virginia City

Distance from downtown Reno
- 50 miles
Phone Number
- (775) 847-0281
Website
- www.jour.unr.edu/outpost/ destinations/archives/ des.pines.graves3.html
Admission Fee
- None
Directions
- Take Virginia Street to Interstate 80. Head east to Highway 395 and south to Carson City. Take Highway 395 south, to the Mount Rose Interchange, following the signs to Virginia City. After you exit the freeway on the large loop, you'll be traveling on Virginia Street. Turn left at the signal onto State Highway 341, the Geiger Grade. Continue on Geiger Grade as it winds up the mountain past stunning displays of red and orange rocks, to Virginia City, about 13 miles. As you enter Virginia City, you'll see a sign for the cemeteries pointing left. Turn left and follow the signs; make another left onto a dirt road; pass the Virginia City RV Park; and find the parking area at the end of the dirt road, the cemeteries will be in front of you.

in the stark hills around Virginia City if you are looking for a strenuous hike but a more memorable dog walk is in the Virginia City cemeteries. There are sandy paths through the widely spaced tombstones marking graves in the stony ground. Many of the graves are protected by elaborate wrought iron fencing or wooden picket fences. A jeep road from the end of the parking area winds down into 7-Mile Canyon where you will find the old Jewish Cemetery, marked by a Star of David and banished to the far side of cemetery hill.

Dog Friendliess

Dogs are allowed to explore the Virginia City cemeteries.

Traffic

You will be joined on this off-beat canine hike by many visitors in the summer, some of whom spend hours reading old headstones.

Canine Swimming

There is no chance for dog paddling in Virginia City.

Trail Time

Less than an hour.

There are 50 more great places to take your dog in the Reno-Lake Tahoe area, but before I get to that, here is a list of parks - thankfully short - that don't allow dogs...

No Dogs!

RENO
Bowers' Mansion Park
The May Arboretum in Rancho San Rafael
Any turf areas at Rancho San Rafael

LAKE TAHOE
D.L. Bliss State Park
(no dogs on trails, beaches or at Vinkingsholm)
Donner Memorial
(no dogs on trails or beaches)
Sugar Pine Point
(no dogs on trails)
Pope, Baldwin, Nevada and Camp Richardson beaches
Heavenly Valley Ski Resort

CARSON VALLEY
Mormon Station State Historic Park

Most California state parks in the area
allow dogs in the campgrounds and improved areas,
but not on the trails.

50 More Places To Hike With Your Dog In The Reno-Lake Tahoe Region

64-Acres Park

Tahoe City
Placer County
located just south of the "Y" in Tahoe City

64-Acres Park is U.S. Forest Service land that is developed, operated and maintained by the Tahoe City Public Utilities District. The park has picnic tables, and accesses the Lakeside Trail 1A between the park and Fanny Bridge. This pleasant trail includes a scenic overlook, benches and rest areas. There is also dogpaddling in the Truckee River.

Ambrose Park

Reno
Washoe County
on River Lane

Ambrose Park offers day-use fishing access to the Truckee River. This part of the river is a great spot for bird watching and your dog may even spy an industrious beaver.

Big Meadow

Luther Pass
United States Forest Service land
Highway 89 (Luther Pass)

This short, one-mile hike is an easy ramble after tackling the first 1/4 mile, which is steep. The trail flattens out by the time it reaches Big Meadow, a jumping off point for detours to one of several lakes in the area. Lake Dardanelles is a favorite destination, a 7-mile round trip involving a moderate to steep hike.

Bijou Community Park

South Lake Tahoe
El Dorado County
1201 Al Tahoe Boulevard

A highlight of this local park is Tahoe's first disc golf course, a stop on the Pro Disc Golf Association Tour. Also on the grounds are a fitness trail and child's playground. There is plenty of room to romp with your dog.

Cold Springs Park

Reno
Washoe County
off Highway 395 on Reno Park Boulevard

This neighborhood park features open spaces and acres of dog-friendly turf. You'll also find a children's playground, horseshoe pits, a jogging trail and volleyball courts. There is a skateboard park, too.

Coon Street Beach

King's Beach
Placer County
at the end of Coon Street, on the east side of King's Beach

This small dog beach is a very popular spot for North Lake Tahoe dogs. You'll find dogs swimming in Lake Tahoe, or trotting along the sandy beach. Try a walk along this beach in the fall, when the shore is deserted and the aspens are turning bright yellow.

Cove East

South Lake Tahoe
El Dorado County
on Venice Drive off Tahoe Keys Boulevard

This short path in Tahoe Keys is a leg-stretcher on paw-friendly sand for up to two miles. The busiest wetlands in the Sierra Nevadas are at the mouth of the Upper Truckee River.

Deer Park

Sparks
City of Sparks
on Prater and Rock boulevards

Deer Park is a pleasant neighborhood park where you can enjoy covered picnic tables, lush mature landscaping, and cement nail-grinding walking paths for the dog. The paths are also lighted for those summertime late evening walks.

Desert Winds

Sparks
Washoe County
105 Ember Drive in the Spanish Springs area

This new 10-acre park was designed for Washoe County by a private developer. It has paved walking trails, picnic tables and horseshoe pits.

Diamond Peak

Incline Village
Washoe County
Diamond Peak ski resort

This is a 1.3-mile hike with a 700-foot rise leading to a scenic picnic spot above Lake Tahoe. The hike leads from Diamond Peak Ski Resort's base lodge to Snowflake Lodge, over a dirt - and sometimes stony - trail along the quad chairs.

Dog Beach

Tahoe City
Placer County
south on Highway 89 at unpaved parking area

There really isn't a name for this rocky beach in Tahoe City, but dogs congregate here, because it's a perfect beach for a doggie aquatics. There is also a paved bike trail parallel to the beach.

Dollar Point Bike Path

Tahoe City
Placer County
on Highway 89

This 2 1/2-mile section of paved multi-use trail is mostly flat with an easy 1/2-mile climb up to Dollar Point. This trail also gives access to Burton Creek State Park, Skylandia Park, Lake Forest Beach, Lake Forest Boat Ramps and Campgrounds, Pomin Park, and Tahoe State Park.

Donnelly Park

Reno
Washoe County
3295 Mayberry Drive in southwest Reno

Donnelly Park is a scenic 30-acre neighborhood oasis donated by the Caughlin family. Here you'll find landscaped grounds, walking trails, benches and spectacular views of the Sierra Nevada. A large 20-acre irrigated pasture invites visitors to experience a bit of Reno's ranching heritage in the Truckee Meadows.

Dorostkar Park

Reno
Washoe County
on Mayberry Drive in southwest Reno

The primary attractions of Dorostkar Park for canine hikers are an interpretive nature trail, a paved bike path and access to the Truckee River.

Eagle Rock

Homewood
United State Forest Service
on Blackwood Canyon Road, off Highway 89

This hike begins on Blackwood Canyon Road, four miles south of Tahoe City on Highway 89. Turn right onto Blackwood Canyon Road and the trail starts 1/4-mile down the road on the left. Just past Homewood look on the left side of the highway for an enormous rock formation and you have discovered Eagle Rock, the neck of an eroded basaltic volcano. The hike to the formation is 1 1/2-miles round-trip, with incredible views.

Elizabeth Williams Park

West Shore
Placer County
north of Kaspian Campground on Highway 89, south of Tahoe City

Fishermen make the most use of this lovely little park. It is a perfect spot to relax on the shore of Lake Tahoe, and let the dog jump in the water. The park is administered by the Tahoe City Public Utilities Division.

Fisherman's Park

Reno
City of Reno
495 Galetti Way

This is a scenic relaxing park located on the Truckee River. There is a shady paved asphalt bike path that runs along the river, so you have a chance to do some wading, too.

Floating Island Lake

South Shore
United StatesForest Service
trailhead on Highway 89 at the Mt. Tallac trailhead

A wide, woody path leads to unique Floating Island Lake where a large grass island actually floats inside the lake. The trail uses switchbacks to soften the 700-foot elevation gain on the 1.5-mile linear trail. You can hike past Floating Island Lake to Cathedral Lake in less than a mile - with another 500 feet of climbing. Further on, 2.6 miles and more than 2,000 feet higher, is the top of Mt. Tallac. Or you can remain at Floating Island Lake and just admire the lofty peak.

Gator Swamp Park

Sparks
Washoe County
255 Egyptian Drive; in the Spanish Springs area

This neighborhood park has a walking path for sedate canine hikers. Operated in conjunction with the Alyce Taylor Elementary School, this park is busy during school recess periods.

Golden Valley Park

Reno
Washoe County
on Hillview Way off Estates Road

Walking trails in this small park are flavored with long views of the mountains and valleys. You'll also find some covered picnic tables, tennis courts and a horse arena.

Granite Lake

Lake Tahoe West Shore
United States Forest Service
Bayview Campground on Highway 89

This a hardy climb for the experienced canine hiker but your work on this switchbacking trail buys you splendid lake views of Emerald Bay and Tahoe. The hike to Granite Lake is two miles round trip and the going gets tougher still to Maggies Peak beyond. This is a round trip of four miles. The damage you see in the fir forest was caused by Bark Beetles during the drought of the early 1990s.

Grass Lake Meadows

Fallen Leaf Lake
United StatesForest Service
Fallen Leaf Road off Highway 89

Grass Lake is one of the overlooked hikes in the Desolation Wilderness. It is an easy 8-mile round trip that you can effort-lessly turn into an overnight hike. Take along some mosquito repellent - and don't forget to spray the dog.

Hidden Valley Park

Reno
Washoe County
4740 Parkway Drive

This is a roomy 480-acre park, only 65 of which are developed. This regional playground caters to horses and equestrians but there are several trail areas for canine hikers to enjoy as well.

Highland Ranch Park

Sun Valley
Washoe County
Highland Ranch Parkway at top of Sun Valley

This neighborhood park in northeast Sun Valley has access to BLM land for hiking and tremendous views of both the Sierra Nevada and the Spanish Springs Valley. There is a dirt walking trail marked by rocks and boulders to follow along the road.

Horsetail Falls

Lake Tahoe
United States Forest Service
US 50 near Twin Bridges

Horsetail Falls is easily visible from the road but canine hikers will want to pull over and climb to the top of the water spout. The trail is only 1 1/2 miles but can be challenging. An alternative is to stop and relax along Pyramid Creek or take the short loop hike with a view of the falls.

Hunter Creek Trail
Reno
United States Forest Service
off Mountaingate in the Juniper Heights subdivision

This is a popular 5-mile round trip that gains 1,000 feet in elevation and affords panoramic views of the city and surrounding hills. The unmaintained trail is not the easiest under paw and you'll need to ford a couple of small creeks, climb rocky ridges and pull up a steep canyon. Look for beaver ponds along the creek.

Incline Village Bikeway
Incline Village
Washoe County
on Lake Tahoe

A network of 7.2 miles of bike paths (19 miles are planned) knot Incline Village together. As of this writing, you can ride from Lakeshore Boulevard from Village Boulevard to Tahoe Boulevard. The paved asphalt path is excellent for dog walking too.

Kilner Park
Tahoe City
Placer County
on Highway 89 & Ward Avenue

This 7-acre pocket park is adjacent to the west shore bike trail, and features several wooded paths to enjoy with your dog. There are also picnic tables and tennis and volleyball courts. This park is administered by the North Tahoe Public Utility District.

Lam Watah Washoe Heritage Site
South Lake Tahoe City
U.S. Forest Service
trailhead is just past corner of US 50 and Kahle Drive

This small archaeological site includes many boulders with depressions where native Washo women ground nuts and grains and prepared food for their families during the summer and processed dried food for the winter. The site is nestled in a lovely meadow like the areas where the Washos spent their summers. The meadow lies along a one-mile hike to Nevada Beach. Your dog can't enjoy the beach, but you can both enjoy the trail.

Manzanita Park
Reno
City of Reno
on Manzanita Street East of Lakeside Drive

This large neighborhood park has something for everyone, including a child's playground, two tennis courts, covered picnic tables and a large grassy area perfect for a quick game of Frisbee with your dog. To conserve water, drought-tolerant grasses are used over most of the park. There are also cement pathways throughout the park.

Mayberry Park
Reno
Washoe County
off Woodland Avenue on Old Highway 40

A peaceful shady spot, Mayberry Park offers a paved asphalt trail and Truckee River access for doggie paddling. The park is also wheelchair accessible, and you can enjoy excellent bird-watching opportunities.

Mira Loma Park

Reno
City of Reno
on Mira Loma Drive at South McCarran Boulevard

Mira Loma Park sits in the heart of the southeast Reno neighborhood known as Donner Springs. Mira Loma Park also features a fitness trail, where joggers can mix in some exercises while squiring the dog. The paths are lighted for nighttime leg-stretchers.

Mogul Park

Reno
Washoe County
on Mogul Mountain Drive off Interstate 80

At Mogul Park you'll find a neighborhood park with a fitness course and pedestrian trail, all against the beautiful backdrop of the Sierras and Truckee River Canyon. There is also a nice lawn area for a spirited game of fetch.

Nevada Shoreline

Sand Harbor
Washoe County
at paved parking lot on Highway 28, 2.9 miles south of Sand Harbor

This is an easy hike of four miles that only climbs 300 feet. The sandy trail follows the shoreline south of Incline Village, past Chimney Beach, Secret Harbor and Whale Beach. Eventually, you'll connect with a service road you can follow back to the parking area.

North Tahoe Regional Park
North Lake Tahoe
Placer County
on National Avenue in Kings Beach

This scenic regional park in North Lake Tahoe is operated by the Tahoe City Public Utility District. There are large grassy areas for playing with your dog, interpretive trails, a bike path, and sandy beaches. The park backs up to Forest Service lands, so you can hike those trails too. There are also winter cross-country ski trails and sledding areas here.

North Valleys Park
Stead
Washoe County
8085 Silver Lake Road

This park is located in the North Valleys Regional Sports Complex (NVRSC) north of Reno in the community of Stead. The trails offer a lovely panorama of high desert open space. You'll also find a community center, skateboard park, children's play area and picnic area in this 160 acres of open space.

Paige Meadow
Tahoe City
United States Forest Service
Forest Service Road 15N60 or 16N48 off Pineland Drive

This is a wonderful springtime hike to take just after the snow melts and the flowers are in bloom. There are really no designated trails, just many footpaths across several beautiful meadows where you can wander among hundreds of wildflowers.

Petersen Mountain

Reno
Bureau of Land Management land
on Red Rock Road in the North Valley area of Reno

Petersen Mountain is a pristine hiking experience very close to Reno, only 30 minutes away. There are numerous trails on the mountain, much of which is protected from roads. Canine hikers can find any level of challenge here, from easy to strenuous. Look for the migratory Lassen-Washoe deer herd if you hike late in the year, they make their winter home on Petersen.

Phillip-Annie Callahan Park

Galena
Washoe County
end of Callahan Ranch Road, off Mount Rose Highway

This park site was once an irrigated pasture surrounded by towering black pines that whisper when the wind blows. The main trail through this new neighborhood park is a wide concrete pathway that winds along babbling Galena Creek. The trail isn't more than half a mile, but dead ends in the forest, where you can continue exploring with your dog. Callahan Park, with views of Mount Rose and Slide Mountain to the west, received the 1999 Elmer H. Anderson Award from the Nevada Parks and Recreation Society.

Pond Peak

Wadsworth
United States Forest Service
town of Olinghouse, east of Sparks and north of Wadsworth

Pond Peak is the third highest peak (8,035) in the Pah Rah Range. The trail to Pond Peak is only four miles round trip from Olinghouse, a small mining town that still has residents. The trail is moderate to difficult, and your dog may pick up a few pebbles in her paws. You'll see some wonderful desert views as you hike this trail.

Pah Rah Park

Sparks
City of Sparks
on Vista Boulevard in east Sparks

Next to Jerry Whitehead Elementary School in east Sparks, Pah Rah Park is a perfect small-town neighborhood park. The large open grass area makes a great place for a game of fetch and the maze of lighted paths have enough hills to craft a sporty canine hike.

Sardine Valley

Truckee
United States Forest Service
Henness Pass Road at Davies Campground

This loop trail is a favorite of mountain bikers, but it makes a nice easy walk with your dog, too. Some of this trail is jeep road, so you may run into some vehicular traffic. Not as scenic as some other Tahoe trails, but you get good views of Sardine Valley.

Silver Knolls Park

Silver Knolls
Washoe County
on West Silver Knolls Boulevard off Red Rock Road

This pocket park seems to appear out of nowhere in the sandy desert. It features picnic tables, horse trails, a horse arena, a playground area and a good variety of hiking trails for you and your dog.

Sugar Pine Point State Park
Tahoe City
Placer County
on West Shore Boulevard

Dogs are not allowed on Sugar Pine Point trails but canine hikers can access a 9-mile section of paved bike trail that runs along West Shore Boulevard. There is some walking on the highway shoulder and residential streets which you may want to avoid, and there are some moderately steep grades along the way.

Tahoe Vista Bike Trail
Tahoe Vista
6600 Donner Road

This short 1-mile walk begins at the end of the parking lot in North Tahoe Regional Park. The path runs up National Avenue through the woods to Pinedrop Street, ending up at Highway 267.

Thomas Creek
Reno
United StatesForest Service
Mount Rose Highway

This is a strenuous hike for canine hikers out for a challenge. It is a 6-mile round trip that rises almost 2000 feet. Along the way you'll see some thick aspen and shade, and some parts of the trail can be under water.

Virginia Foothills Park
Virginia Foothills
Washoe County
off Mira Loma Road

Located next to Brown Elementary School, this 11-acre park features a fitness trail, walking paths and a children's playground. Walk in this neighborhood park and enjoy views of Geiger Grade and the Virginia Range.

Whitaker Park
Reno
City of Reno
on University Terrace off Ralston Street

Dog owners will come to this small residential park for its dog park or a quick leg-stretcher around the perimeter of the landscaped grounds. Some of the houses in the surrounding neighborhoods are among the oldest buildings in Reno.

Wilson Commons Park
Washoe Valley
Washoe County
on Susan Lee Circle, on the west side of Washoe Valley

This beautiful park is part open space, and part history lesson. You can view a 100-year old barn and ranch outbuildings, 20 acres of irrigated pasture, and several acres of developed parkland. The developed portion features a fishing pond and benches for viewing the impressive Sierra Nevada.

Wingfield Park

Reno
City of Reno
at First and Arlington in downtown Reno

Five downtown parks have joined to make Wingfield Park — Wingfield Park (East Island), Brick Park, Bennett Park, Wingfield Park (West Island) and Bicentennial Park. Wingfield Park remembers political power broker George Wingfield, who came to Reno to dig for gold and ended up building banks and hotels. The parks offer peaceful benches, tennis courts, an amphitheatre used throughout the years, and part of the Truckee River Path, along with other pathways and large grassy areas.

Dog Parks and Dog Beaches in The Reno/Lake Tahoe Region

Dog Parks

Dog parks often begin as informal gatherings of dog owners that eventaully become legitimized by local government. Here are several in the Reno/Lake Tahoe region:

▶ **Sparks Marina Park** (Sparks; see page 38)

▶ **Whitaker Park** (Reno; see page 133)

▶ **Village Green** (Lake Tahoe; see page 106)

▶ **Virginia Lake Park** (Reno; see page 36)

Tips for enjoying your visit to the dog park

🐾 Keep an eye on your dog and a leash in hand. Situations can change quickly in a dog park.

🐾 Keep puppies younger than 4 months at home until they have all necessary innoculations to allow them to play safely with other dogs. Make certain that your older dog is current on shots and has a valid license.

🐾 ALWAYS clean up after your dog. Failure to pick up your dog's poop is the quickest way to spoil a dog park for everyone.

🐾 If your dog begins to play too rough, don't take time to sort out blame - leash the dog and leave immediately.

🐾 Leave your female dog at home if she is in heat.

🐾 Don't volunteer to bring all the dogs in the neighborhood with you when you go. Don't bring any more dogs than you can supervise comfortably.

🐾 Observe and follow all posted regulations at the dogpark.

🐾 **HAVE AS MUCH FUN AS YOUR DOG!**

Dog Beaches

Dog parks often restricted from "people" beaches, especially in-season. Here are several beaches in the Reno/Lake Tahoe region that welcome your dog:

▶ **Coon Street Beach** (Lake Tahoe; see page 119)

▶ **"Dog" Beach** (Tahoe City; see page 121)

▶ **Kiva Beach** (Lake Tahoe; see page 55)

▶ **Sparks Marina Park** (Sparks; see page 38)

Tips For Taking Your Dog To The Beach

🐾 The majority of dogs can swim and love it, but dogs entering the water for the first time should be tested; never throw your dog into the water. Start in shallow water and call your dog's name - or try to coax him in with a treat or toy. Always keep your dog within reach.

🐾 Another way to introduce your dog to the water is with a dog that already swims and is friendly with your dog. Let your dog follow his friend.

🐾 If your dog begins to doggie paddle with his front legs only, lift his hind legs and help him float. He should quickly catch on and will keep his back end up.

- Swimming is a great form of exercise, but don't let your dog overdo it. He will be using new muscles and may tire quickly.

- Dogs can get sunburned, especially short-haired breeds and ones with pink skin and white hair. Limit your dog's exposure when the sun is strong and apply sunblock to his ears and nose 30 minutes before going outside.

- If your dog is out of shape, don't encourage him to run on the sand. Running on the beach is strenuous exercise and a dog that is out of shape can easily pull a tendon or ligament.

Index To Parks and Trails

141

About The Author

Sherril Steele-Carlin lived and worked at Grand Canyon National Park's South Rim for two years. Living and working in a national park gave her a great appreciation for the beauty of all of our parks, and their place in our lives. She loves to share the beauty of the outdoors with all her animals!

Today, she's a full-time freelance writer, living about an hour away from another great natural wonder, Lake Tahoe. She's published numerous articles in print publications like *Rock & Gem, The Original Farmer's Almanac, American Profile, Nevada Magazine, Cat Fancy,* and many others. She also writes for several web sites including About.com (www.renotahoe.about.com).

Sherril has previously turned her life experiences into two e-books: *How to Get a Life by Living and Working in a National Park* and *How to Break Into Casino Jobs.*

COMING IN 2004...

The Canine Hikers Bible: A Companion for the Active Dog Owner

- ☛ descriptions of over 100 dog-friendly parks in popular destinations
- ☛ canine hikes in 25 of North America's largest cities
- ☛ beach rules for dogs at over 1300 beaches in 500+ beach towns
- ☛ rules for dogs in 102 of the most visited national park lands
- ☛ 15 towns canine hikers will love

Cruden Bay Books publishes guidebooks for canine hikers in communities around North America. For more information on A BARK IN THE PARK books please visit our website at **www.hikewithyourdog.com**. At the site you can find:

- ▸ direct links to more than 2000 dog-friendly parks
- ▸ recommendations for favorite hikes and can share your favorite hike with your dog with others
- ▸ tip sheets for going on a hike with your dog
- ▸ and much more

Cruden Bay Books
PO Box 467
Montchanin, DE 19710
Phone: 302-999-8843
Fax: 302-326-0400
E-mail: crubay@earthlink.net
www.hikewithyourdog.com

Want to order A BARK IN THE PARK books for your organization? Quantity discounts available.